D1610337

C333029753

VICHY
AIR FORCE
AT WAR

VICHY
AIR FORCE
AT WAR

The French Air Force that fought the Allies in World War II

Jonathan Sutherland
& Diane Canwell

Pen & Sword
AVIATION

First published in Great Britain in 2011 by
PEN & SWORD AVIATION
An imprint of
Pen & Sword Books Ltd
47 Church Street
Barnsley
South Yorkshire
S70 2AS

ISBN 978-1-84884-336-3

A CIP catalogue record for this book is available from the British Library.

Typeset by Concept, Huddersfield, West Yorkshire
Printed and bound in England by CPI UK.

Pen & Sword Books Ltd incorporates the Imprints of Pen & Sword Aviation,
Pen & Sword Maritime, Pen & Sword Military, Wharncliffe Local History,
Pen & Sword Select, Pen & Sword Military Classics, Leo Cooper,
Remember When, Seaforth Publishing and Frontline Publishing

For a complete list of Pen & Sword titles please contact
PEN & SWORD BOOKS LIMITED
47 Church Street, Barnsley, South Yorkshire, S70 2AS, England
E-mail: enquiries@pen-and-sword.co.uk
Website: www.pen-and-sword.co.uk

Contents

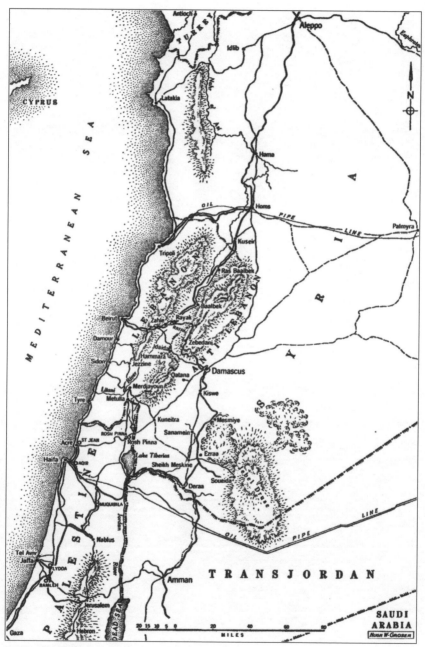

The Middle-East Theatre.

Introduction

Collaboration is often seen as a dirty, loaded word. Yet it can be argued that the actions of the Vichy regime after the defeat and partial occupation of France in 1940 is nothing other than that. Collaboration means cooperation. It also suggests support and assistance. Certainly, the Vichy regime encouraged not only co-operation, but outright belligerence and armed resistance towards their former allies, notably the British. The Vichy regime of Pétain and Laval, in particular, believed that in collaborating with Germany and Hitler they could avoid the worst depredations of occupation and that France could emerge from the chaos of the defeat in May 1940 as an independent partner in a stronger Europe.

As far as de Gaulle's Free French were concerned, the Vichy regime regarded them as little more than renegades, British puppets and would-be usurpers. The situation that France found itself in after the German invasion in May 1940 was unenviable. Paul Renaud's government collapsed in the aftermath of the defeat, and on 17 June 1940 Philippe Pétain (considered to be an outstanding leader in the First World War and a French military hero) set about establishing a solid political relationship with Germany.

The first step would be an armistice, primarily to avoid unnecessary bloodshed, and then to establish a better working arrangement with Germany. At this stage, as far as Pétain and his confederates were concerned, Britain could not hope to stand alone. Germany would be the dominant power in Europe and France had to seek accommodations to live with that reality.

With the armistice signed, Pétain's government needed a new capital. Paris and most of France was under occupation. After some debate, Vichy, a small spa town, was chosen. This was ideally situated as it was close to the border of the occupied and unoccupied zones of France. The town also had a number of hotels that could be pressed into service as accommodation for the new government.

Pétain and his ministers were certain that France, as a colonial power and a major player in Europe, would be well placed to become an important ally to the Germans. The *L'État français* (French State) was formally created on 12 July 1940. Pétain met with Hitler at Montoire-sur-le-Loire in central France on 24 October, having already used the word 'collaboration' in a radio broadcast earlier in the month.

As far as Pétain and Laval were concerned, they were prepared to acknowledge Germany as the dominant force in Europe and hoped that this acceptance could secure special concessions from the Germans. One immediate concern was the swift release of an estimated 1.6 million French prisoners of war being held by the Germans. Equally important was the safety of the French population in the occupied zone and the hope that the Germans would accept lower levels of indemnities than they were demanding in the aftermath of the defeat. There was also the question of sovereignty of the Vichy regime over the occupied and unoccupied zones of France.

Pétain and Laval saw collaboration as essential in being able to ensure that the Vichy regime had time to reconstruct France, to complete their National Revolution and sweep away the last vestiges of the discredited Third Republic. A degree of collaboration was expected under Article 3 of the armistice convention that France had been compelled to sign. France was obliged to cooperate with the German occupation forces. The Germans had the right of veto on appointments and policy. Without doubt, the fact that the Germans were occupying vast areas of France and still held the prisoners was instrumental in ensuring that France collaborated. The Vichy regime was dependent on the Germans; all Vichy could do was to dress collaboration as French initiatives. The notorious *Statut des Juifs*, anti-Semitic legislation, is a prime example of this.

In reality, the majority of Germans had no intention of treating the French as equals. There were Francophiles in important positions, such as the Foreign Secretary von Ribbentrop and the German ambassador to Vichy France, Otto Abetz. For the most part, however, France was now seen as a supplier of vital war materials and labour. Herman Göring (commander in chief of the *Luftwaffe* since 1935) took this view, typical of many high-ranking Germans with influence; he advocated the economic exploitation of France.

Josef Goebbels, the German Minister for Propaganda, claimed that it was his desire to see France as little more than an 'enlarged Switzerland', in effect a tourist destination and a maker of high-quality clothing.

As far as Hitler was concerned, he saw the collaboration in a far more pragmatic way. By encouraging it, France was kept permanently out of the war and it would mean, in time, that France would police itself and defend its own borders from the British and Allies. He was not concerned about creating a Nazi-style state in France; he was too concerned with his own agenda for Germany.

France would become very important to the Germans, particularly the industrial sector, which had a large and efficient coal and steel industry as well aircraft and motor vehicle manufacturers. Private companies feared that if they did not collaborate and produce war materials for the Germans then their assets would be seized by the occupiers. Some were less than scrupulous and saw business opportunities, such as the photographic company Photomaton, which offered to produce identity cards for Jews being held in concentration camps.

In the first two years of the occupation, French output and profits increased as businesses eagerly signed lucrative contracts with the Germans. The cooperation also meant an opportunity to modernize. The commonly held belief is that the post-war years saw the modernization of European manufacturing out of the chaos, destruction and ashes of the war. In fact, the modernization of French industry began during the war itself, particularly in the field of aircraft production.

According to the Eton-educated, Austrian-born, British historian David Pryce-Jones, around 8,000,000 to 9,000,000 French worked directly for the Germans in some capacity. It is certainly the case that by the beginning of 1942, the supply of manpower from Russia and Poland had begun to run out. It fell on the Nazi Fritz Sauckel (General Plenipotentiary for Labour Deployment) to find new 'recruits' for German industry. In May 1942 he demanded that the

French send some 250,000 workers to Germany by the end of July 1942.

Laval responded by setting up a scheme known as *'la relève'*. Under the scheme, for every three workers sent to Germany, the Germans would release one French prisoner of war. Unfortunately for Laval and for the French prisoners of war, the scheme was not met with universal acclaim and volunteers were in short supply. As a consequence of this the Vichy administration was forced to introduce a version of conscription in February 1943. This new scheme, known as *le Service du Travail Obligatoire* (STO) was to have other unwanted consequences for Laval and the Vichy regime.

Increasing numbers of *réfractaires* (passive resisters) were created, comprising mainly the young. A large number of them joined the resistance movement and others attempted to get jobs in mining and other exempt occupations. Nonetheless, a large number of French men and women did find themselves in Germany working as un-skilled labour. After Poland, France provided the largest numbers for labour; it has been estimated that upwards of 650,000 French men and 44,000 French women were working in Germany during the war.

France also provided considerable wealth to Germany during the war, a conservative estimate being around 40 per cent. In 1940, for example, the Vichy regime authorized the transfer of the Belgian gold reserves to Germany as well as the shares to the valuable Bohr copper mine in Yugoslavia. The Vichy regime was also complicit in looting art, antiques and other valuables from French Jews, the items or the proceeds from which were all sent to Germany.

On a daily basis there was fairly widespread collaboration. Many letters and notes were written either to the Vichy or German author-ities, which identified members of the resistance or their sympa-thizers, those that were avoiding conscription, black marketers and, of course, Jews. Collaborationist magazines and newspapers were very popular, with up to 300,000 readers per title. Many of the letters denouncing individuals had far more to do with personal grudges than ideology, but, nonetheless, this still amounted to a form of collaboration.

In this book we focus primarily on the conflicts that had to be fought against the Vichy French around the Mediterranean and beyond. Vichy had tried to tread the line between neutrality, self-defence and the beginnings of a new relationship with Germany. This became increasingly more difficult. The Second World War is often referred to as the first total war. Certain French colonies and territories were strategically placed and therefore of value to Germany and her allies, as well as to Britain and her own supporters. Vichy did offer various forms of support toward the German war effort, a prime example being that offered by Admiral Darlan, who offered Germany logistical support in both Tunisia and in Syria.

Other, more overt, attempts to integrate French armed forces with the *Wehrmacht* were rejected; a prime example is that of the French offer to create a *Légion Tricolore*, effectively French troops in French uniforms, to fight in Tunisia. The offer was rejected. The Germans often found it difficult to reconcile their differing views of France. On the one hand France was, of course, a conquered territory, but on the other the Vichy regime made offers of support very much in the same mould as an ally.

In this book it will become clear that many of the actions fought against the Vichy French were initiated by Britain. So in this respect, Vichy's priority of defence meant resisting any attempt to invade any of its colonies. It was inevitable then, despite the fact that the Vichy regime wanted to remain neutral, that it would come into conflict on the battlefield, in the skies and at sea, with the Allies.

There are other areas of collaboration and assistance that fall outside of the parameters of this book. On 22 July 1943 Frenchmen were given permission to join the *Waffen SS*. In the same year Laval gave permission to create the *Milice*. This organization was hated throughout France and many of its members were either lynched or executed after France had been liberated. It was the *Milice* that collaborated closely with the German military occupation forces in hunting down and killing members of the resistance.

There were many collaborationist groups and parties, even in the occupied zone of France, such as the *Légion des Volontaires Français Contre le Bolchevisme* or more simply *Légion des Volontaires Français* (LVF). Initially, there were around 10,000 volunteers who fought on the Eastern Front in German uniforms against the Russians. Even after the liberation of France many of these men continued to fight on beside the Germans, as part of the SS Charlemagne Division.

The justification for collaboration put forward by Laval and others in the Vichy regime was that it would reduce the damage that would be caused by the German occupation. Pétain used this very argument in his trial after the war. He claimed that he, along with the Vichy regime, had created a shield that had protected France against the worst excesses of the German occupation. They may well have truly believed this to have been the case, but the evidence does not support their claim. The Vichy regime's understanding of the German policy was limited. Vichy had also assumed that Germany had won the war in Europe. Finally, it was clear that they did not recognize how much Germany had changed by 1940 compared with the state that had been forced to sign an armistice back in 1918.

Vichy collaborationists also argued that their actions had prevented France from becoming another Poland. In Poland there had been wholesale slaughter, resettlement and asset stripping. The process of Polonization had certainly taken place in France from 1940; upwards of 80,000 Jews had been deported, 750,000 French men and women had been forcibly deported to work in Germany, around 135,000 French had been put on trial and at least 70,000 'enemies of the state' had been interned. Throughout all of this the French police and the *Milice* were excessive in suppressing the resistance.

The way in which France behaved post-1940 is in stark contrast to the behaviour of Holland. In the Netherlands, civil servants were only expected to ensure that essential services continued to function; they did not provide any further assistance to the Germans.

France and Britain had stood together through adversity and to ultimate victory in the First World War. In 1939 they both declared war on Germany, following her refusal to withdraw from Poland. Once again, the British Expeditionary Force and supporting units from the Royal Air Force and the Royal Navy were mobilized to protect Western Europe. This time there was to be no stalemate, no long-term solidarity against a common foe. Although for the first nine months of the war there would be little action in Europe, when it did come it was swift, brutal and decisive. France would be over-run and the British forces, or at least what remained of them, were plucked from the coast of France to return to Britain to lick their wounds. The *Entente Cordiale* had been severely damaged and over the coming months it would be broken.

France did not launch attacks against the British Isles, yet they resisted her and sought to retrieve their own honour by launching attacks whenever possible. The conflicts would come in the Middle East and in West and North Africa. Ultimately, the Vichy regime would be swept aside and a new voice of France, Charles de Gaulle, would emerge as an unwilling yet pragmatic ally of Britain. Those that had led the Vichy regime and many of those who had fought for it would be shunned, imprisoned or executed, while many others jumped ship and became Free French as soon as they saw that the tide of the war had inevitably turned against Germany.

The French faced the German invasion of 1940 with 4,360 modern combat aircraft and with 790 new machines arriving from French and American factories each month. When the Phony War finally ended, some 119 of 210 squadrons were ready for action on the north-eastern front. The others were re-equipping or stationed in the colonies. The 119 squadrons could bring into action only a quarter of the aircraft available.

The French Air Force was conceived as a defensive arm, in co-operation with or attached to the ground troops. At the time of the German attack the French Air Force was just modernizing and reorganizing.

With France overrun by June 1940, what remained of the French Air Force was either concentrated in the unoccupied zone or had been hastily redeployed to the colonies. Nonetheless, in retaliation for the British attack on the French fleet in Oran, French bombers, based in French Morocco, carried out retaliatory air raids over Gibraltar.

The *Armée de l'Air de Vichy* was born and would fight to the best of its ability against their former allies in theatres as distant as north-west Africa, Syria, Lebanon, Madagascar and the Far East. Not only would they take to the skies against the British and later the Americans, they would also willingly take part in aerial duels against Free French pilots.

A handful of books have been written on French aircraft, but never has there been a complete history of the operations of the

Vichy Air Force and its fratricidal war. This title literally spans the globe, examining forgotten air combats. It is also important to note that many of the Vichy pilots that survived the air combats later volunteered to join the Free French and would fight with great courage and distinction alongside the very pilots that they had been trying to kill.

This is very much a missing piece of the Second World War air war. Many believe that the French Air Force virtually ceased to exist after the 1940 armistice. This book will provide for the first time the actions and operations against former allies and their grim determination to protect the remnants of the French empire, whilst allying themselves with their former foes.

All efforts have been made to contact the representatives of the Camouflage Air Club, Marseille, in respect of a number of photographs. We acknowledge that these photographs orginated from the Club, which now appears to have ceased operations.

Chapter One

Armée de l'Air

The first shots that would see conflict between Britain and her erstwhile ally were fired by the French. It was shortly before dawn on Wednesday 3 July 1940. The shots were not fired over the skies of France, nor for that matter were they shot in any sky, but inside a state-of-the-art French submarine, *Surcouf*, which was moored in Devonport. Not only were the first shots fired, but also the first casualties were inflicted. Much had happened before this skirmish inside a blacked-out harbour.

The French aviation industry during the interwar period had built far more military aircraft than any of its foreign competitors. Some 1,500 Breguet 19 bombers (1922) and 3,500 Potez 25 Army Cooperation Aircraft were constructed. Between them they were the most widely used military aircraft in the world – they were extremely robust and reliable. Back in 1927 one of the bombers had flown across the Atlantic. No fewer than thirty of the Potez 25s had circumnavigated Africa in 1933. These were not the only examples of extremely good aircraft. They were famed for their technical excellence and reliability. For a three-year period, from 1924, the fast medium bomber, the Lioré et Olivier 20, beat all-comers. In 1934 the Potez 542 retained the prestigious label as the fastest bomber in Europe for two years. Comparatively speaking, a number of the French aircraft were hugely superior to other bombers being built by European competitors. The Amiot 143, of which the French had eighteen squadrons, could carry a 2-ton bomb load at a speed of 190 mph at just short of 26,000 feet.

The Germans had their Dornier Do23G, which could only carry a 1-ton bomb load. It had a maximum speed of 160 mph and could barely reach 14,000 feet.

The French beat the 30,000 feet ceiling in 1936, with the Bloch 210. It was to be the only aircraft that could reach this height before 1939. The French would eventually equip twenty-four squadrons with this aircraft. The French also had the first modern four-engine heavy bomber, in the Farman 222, built in 1936. It was designed to carry a heavy load of bombs, so it was an ideal night operation aircraft, as comparatively speaking it was slow. They also had the fastest medium bombers in the Amiot 354 (298 mph) and the Lioré et Olivier 451 (307 mph). The Bloch 174 reconnaissance bomber, which was introduced during 1940, had a speed of 329 mph, which made it the fastest multi-engine aircraft in the world. All three of these French aircraft could easily outpace the German equivalents. The fastest the Germans could muster was the Junkers Ju88A, with a top speed of 292 mph. The Dornier Do17K and the Heinkel He111e were upwards of 30 mph slower than this.

It was not just in the bomber field that the French excelled. Their fighters were of excellent quality. Of the twenty-two world airspeed records that were set between the wars, French fighter aircraft held half of them. In fact, the Nieuport-Delage 29 (1921) held seven alone. For four years from 1924 the Gourdou-Leseurre 32 was the fastest operational fighter. This aircraft was only beaten by another French fighter, the Nieuport-Delage 62. The Dewoitine 371 took the record in 1934 and in 1936 the Dewoitine 510 reached a speed of 250 mph, the first operational fighter to do so.

The French fighters were also excellent in other areas of development. In 1935 the Dewoitine 501 became the first fighter with a cannon that could fire through a propeller hub.

Whatever the shortcomings of the French Air Force in 1940, it was not a lack of technical ability, nor indeed, for that matter, lack of numbers. By May 1940 French aircraft manufacturers were producing 619 combat aircraft every month. The French were also buying American aircraft, which were being delivered at a rate of 170 per month.

The French Air Force during the First World War had suffered from the same lack of understanding and poor deployment that the majority of other air forces had experienced during the conflict. On the one hand, the army wanted to have squadrons of aircraft under their direct command. For the aviators themselves, they saw the opportunity to concentrate their forces and deliver crippling blows against the enemy at decisive points on the front line. In the end it was the aviators that won the argument and in April 1918 the 1st Aviation Division was created. It had 585 combat aircraft split up into twenty-four fighter squadrons and fifteen bomber squadrons.

The creation of this unit did not solve all of the problems. Corps and divisional infantry commanders tended to use the assets as protection for their observation aircraft. Like all of the other aviation wings the French Air Force, as it was then, was still a junior partner. The situation began to change after the First World War. The French Government passed two laws in 1928 and in 1933 that effectively created a separate French Air Force. It would no longer be subordinate to either the army or the navy.

In the period 1926 to 1937 the number of squadrons steadily rose to 134. By 1937 there were two air corps and six air divisions. Compromise in terms of command and control of these units was protracted. This meant that the army and the navy, with the connivance of the French Air Ministry, retained operational control of 118 of the squadrons. Thus, only sixteen bomber squadrons were directly under the air force chain of command.

The influence of the army and the navy was even deeper. Back in 1932 the air force had argued for the creation of large, heavily armed aircraft that could engage in bombing, reconnaissance and aerial combat. They were not designed for close cooperative support of any battle on the ground. As a consequence, the army had an undue influence on the type of aircraft chosen and their deployment. In January 1936, of the 2,162 front-line aircraft 63 per cent were primarily observation and reconnaissance aircraft, which would work directly with the army. A further 20 per cent were designed to protect observation aircraft.

Even after disastrous military manoeuvres in 1935, which seemed to indicate that Bloch 200 aircraft were not ideal for attacking motorized columns, there was still refusal to consider introducing dive bombers or assault aircraft. As far as the French Air Force was concerned, it was not their job to attack targets on the battlefield; they were a strategic force. This point of view was supported by the French Air Minister, Pierre Cot (June 1936 to January 1938). He authorized the tripling of the bomber force through acquisition and reorganization. Observation was now the role of air force reserves. This meant that the majority of regular air force units were designated as strategic bombing units. Cot dealt with the opposition from the Superior Air Council by getting the French Parliament to reduce the mandatory retirement age of senior officers. This swept away all of the senior commanders in the French Air Force. Cot simply replaced them with men that supported his own military viewpoint.

The air force was thrown into even greater confusion in 1938 when Guy la Chambre took over from Cot as the air minister. Not only did the new man not agree with this strategic bombing role of the air force and do a u-turn, ensuring that the air force would focus on close support for the army, but he also removed all of the men that Cot had promoted. As a result of this the air force now found itself fighting a secretive war with the government, the air minister and parliament. They simply continued following the strategic bombing approach, while making comforting noises to their opponents.

In their preoccupation with this strategy, vital elements of air warfare were ignored. The airfields were under-funded, command, control and communications were poorly developed and there was a very rudimentary ground-based observer corps. This would ultimately mean that when the French Air Force faced the *Luftwaffe* in 1940 they would find it impossible to track and to intercept incoming streams of enemy aircraft.

The chief of the French Air Force, General Vuillemin, found himself in a very difficult position in January 1939. He was told that in 1940 the aircraft production schedules would provide him with 600 new aircraft per month. Owing to the lack of aircrew and ground crew, Vuillemin responded by saying that he only needed a maximum of sixty per month. In the end he settled for 330, which was forty fewer than the French factories were to produce per month alone. Vuillemin was aware that to expand the training programme would take up almost all of the time and effort of the air force. He called up reservists and many of these men would fly in front-line aircraft, but it was still not enough. Consequently, he began imposing modification requirements on the new aircraft. This meant that newly delivered aircraft were not even commissioned, as they required additional components, such as extra guns and radios. The air staff kept up this ridiculous pretence by instituting incredibly complicated acceptance inspections. American aircraft arriving in crates were simply left in the crates and were never unpacked.

As the French Air Force moved toward combat with Germany in 1940 it had insufficient aircrew and ground staff, a pitiful infrastructure, and secrets to be kept from the government, the air minister, the army and the navy. The net result was that the air force would end up fighting an entirely different war from the army when the Germans launched their attacks in May 1940.

In the early hours of 10 May 1940 three German army groups began an assault on the Low Countries and France. The Germans had a nominal strength of some 3,634 aircraft. Of this total just over 1,000 were fighters, 1,500 were bombers, 500 were reconnaissance aircraft and 550 were transports. The German plan was precisely the same as it had been in Poland – to destroy the Allied air force on the ground.

The French faced the invasion with 4,360 combat aircraft. By this stage 790 new aircraft were being delivered by French and American manufacturers every month. As we have seen, the French Air Force was neither prepared nor organized to cope with these numbers of new aircraft and it was also not organized to fight a war.

Just 119 squadrons were deployed on the north-eastern front. This was out of a total of 210 squadrons. All of the others were either based in the Colonies or were in the process of being re-equipped. This all meant that the combined Allied air force was decidedly weaker than their German counterparts.

If the Germans had expected to catch the French napping, however, they would be sadly mistaken. The Morane 406s of *Groupe de Chasse* II/2, based at Laon-Chambry, attacked incoming Do17s. A pair of Curtiss Hawks out of Suippes engaged Bf110s. Over Verdun, Do17s and their Bf110 escorts were also engaged by Curtiss Hawks. Elsewhere, the Germans were luckier; the Curtiss Hawks of GCII/4 at Xaffevillers suffered a total of six write-offs.

GCII/5, at Toul-Croix de Metz, came under attack from a formation of He111s. The Curtiss Hawks of the French unit were widely dispersed, with some preparing to take off as they had already spotted a reconnaissance flight of Do17s. Two of the Hawks managed to get aloft and engage the German raiders. Meanwhile, at

Norrent-Fontes, Morane 406 fighters engaged a number of He111s, destroying several of them.

Some of the other French units were not as lucky; the *Groupes Aérines d'Observations* (GAO) and *Groupes de Reconnaissance* (GR) were hit particularly hard. A single raid did for all of the aircraft of GAO2/551, while GAO4/551 lost all but three of their nine aircraft in a single raid. At Monceau le Waast, the GRII/33 were attacked by Do17s. They lost one aircraft in the raid and another two were damaged.

With the Germans finally having shown their hand, it quickly became apparent that the key bottleneck would be the Albert Canal in Belgium. German troops had crossed it on the first day of the assault. If the Allies could destroy the bridges across the canal, along with the crossings in the Maastricht area, over the River Maas, this would mean slowing, if not halting, the German advance. The Lioré et Olivier 451s of GBII/12, based at Persan-Beaumont, and those with GBI/12 at Soissons-Saconin were earmarked for the attack. The twelve bombers were escorted by eighteen Morane 406s belonging to GCII/6. The first attack in the morning of 11 May 1940 was unsuccessful; the Germans had brought up flak guns and positioned them around the bridges and there was also German fighter cover. A second attack only succeeded in causing slight damage to one bridge.

On 12 May a French reconnaissance flight over the area stirred up a hornet's nest of German defences. German airborne troops had taken the Vroenhoven and the Veldwezelt bridges across the Albert Canal. Both the RAF and Belgian aircraft had tried to destroy these bridges. The French now threw the assault bomber group, GBAI/54s Breguet 693 twin-engine bombers, at the target. They attacked in three waves of three aircraft. German troops were crossing one of the bridges when the attack came in. The French managed to destroy some German transports, but accomplished little else. The task of dealing with these bridges now passed to the RAF.

On the night of 11/12 May one of GRII/33's Potez reconnaissance aircraft had taken off from the airfield at Athies-sous-Laon. To the horror of the pilot, he spotted that the roads to the south of the River Meuse in the Ardennes region of Belgium were packed with

6

German transports. On the morning of 12 May a second mission was flown and as the Potez 63 approached the small town of Marche the spearhead of a German armoured division was located. From the French aircraft's advantage point German armoured cars and motorcycles could be viewed moving freely across the countryside, directly towards the French border. The Potez, flown by Adjutant Favret, along with an army observer and an air gunner, dropped down to as low as 65 feet and even engaged German ground targets. The crew were not believed when they returned to base and tried to describe what they had seen. Quite simply, the commander of the French 9th Army did not believe them.

A little later, another Potez of GRII/22 spotted German troops crossing the River Semois at Bouillon in Belgium. Once again, their observations were largely ignored, this time by the French 2nd Army. By the time it dawned on the French that what the pilots had seen was not only correct but also highly dangerous, it was too late and the Germans had crossed the River Meuse at Montherne and Sedan. The French Air Force launched waves of bombers against the German motorized columns near Sedan, suffering a number of casualties. German ground losses were particularly high in the area.

On 13 May 1940 came the arrival of the Dewoitine 520. One of the squadrons, GCI/3, entered combat for the first time, shooting down a number of German aircraft, including an He111. For a time the squadron was based at Wez-Thuisy. On the following day the squadron added to their tally, shooting down two Do17s, three Bf110s and a pair of Bf109s. So far, the squadron had only lost one aircraft.

These kinds of kill ratios were replicated across a number of different aircraft types. Certainly, in many instances the kill-to-loss ratio of French to German aircraft was decidedly in the French favour. There were eight squadrons equipped with Curtiss aircraft and they claimed 220 confirmed German aircraft kills for the loss of just thirty-three pilots. In seven major aerial battles, where Curtiss aircraft engaged combinations of Messerschmitt Bf109es and 110cs, the French destroyed twenty-seven of the former and six of the latter for just three aircraft. In the aerial battles that pitched the Morane 406 against Messerschmitts the kill-to-loss ratio was 191 to 89. There were eighteen squadrons equipped with the Morane 406 in May 1940.

Even the Bloch MB150, or 152, which was even faster and more powerful than the Morane, performed extremely well. On 10 May there were twelve squadrons equipped with these fighters and another half a dozen became operational before the campaign was over. The kill-to-loss ratio was again in favour of the French, with 156 to 59.

Whilst the French Air Force was more than holding its own in the skies, the army was suffering disaster after disaster. On 15 May the French 7th Army in Belgium withdrew and the 9th Army practically ceased to exist.

Throughout 16 May the French Air Force threw everything they could at the Germans to halt the advance. It was all in vain, however, as huge numbers of German troops had already crossed the River Meuse. There were now so many conflicting priorities; on the one hand steady retreats, which threatened to turn into routs, had to be covered, while on the other hand the piercing German armoured columns had to be stalled. Added to this were the other targets, which still included bridges and river crossings.

The Germans were still able to launch surprise raids. A prime example took place on 17 May, when German Do17s hit Maubeuge airfield, which was then home to GC2/6. The eighteen Morane 406s were destroyed and just two of their aircraft could be salvaged. French squadrons in forward positions were now beginning to take a severe beating.

Amidst all this chaos, units were still receiving new consignments of aircraft, including Glenn Martin 167s and Douglas DB7s. While some squadrons were receiving long-awaited aircraft, other squadrons were still perilously under strength when they were called into action. GBI/21 and GBII/21 were eagerly awaiting Amiot 354 bombers, but only a handful had arrived when they were ordered to the front line.

Over the period from 22 to 23 May the French Air Force were launching bombing sorties against towns that their army counterparts had recently abandoned. Their mission was to block the main roads with debris. It soon became apparent that one of the key areas in this crucial stage of the war was around Cambrai, Arras and

Amiens. The French Air Force threw everything they could against this region. Attacks were made on German troop concentrations. A notable attack was made on 22 May by Potez 633s of GBAII/51, with just nine available aircraft.

In fact, this aircraft was never meant to be used in France at all. The French Government had decided that all of these aircraft would be sold to foreign air forces. It had come as no great surprise when three Potez 631s were attacked by half a dozen Dewoitine 520 fighters during the evening of 20 May.

The Dewoitine aircraft belonging to GCII/3, based at the tiny airfield at Betz-Bouillancy, engaged a large formation of He111s to the south-west of Senlis on 21 May. No fewer than eight German bombers were shot down here. They, too, made the mistake on their return flight of engaging a Potez 631. One of the Dewoitine fighters buzzed the Potez five times. By this time the pilot of the Potez, Adjutant Martin, was convinced that the French aircraft had probably been captured by a German. His air gunner, Adjutant Guichard, opened fire, shooting down the Dewoitine to the north of Senlis.

There were other incidents such as this, which only serve to prove that communication within the French Air Force was rudimentary to say the least. A Potez was flown from base to base so that all of the French pilots could recognize its configuration.

The French army did try to launch an armoured counter-attack in the Cambrai sector and GCII/3 provided eighteen aircraft as cover on 22 May. They encountered a large number of Ju87s. The air combat began at around 1710 hours and in a matter of minutes eleven of the German dive bombers had been shot down. Suddenly, ten or more Bf109s arrived; they managed to shoot down one of the Dewoitine 520s, a second was lost when it ran out of fuel and a third had to be crash-landed.

The auxiliary units, known as the *Escadrilles Légères de Défense* (ELD), or *Escadrilles de Chasse de Défense* (ECD), had been mobilized on 11 May 1940, although some local defence units were already established. These auxiliary units were mainly reservist pilots. Some of them were test pilots attached to aircraft factories. At the Châteaudun base one of the pilots flying a Bloch 152 shot down a He111 on 12 May. More of these local defence flights were called up to protect aircraft plants. In the majority of cases the aircraft they were flying had come straight off the production line and others were there for repairs. Many of the pilots were not, in fact, French Air Force at all, but were employed by aircraft companies. The majority of the units could muster no more than six aircraft. Most of them flew Bloch fighters, others Morane 406s or Dewoitine 501s and 510s. A number of Dewoitine 500s were also being flown.

One peculiar aircraft that was also used was the Koolhoven FK-58A. It was Dutch built and there were fourteen of them parked at Romorantin. Four of them were sent to Lyons-Bron, where former Polish Air Force pilots were being trained to use French aircraft. The *Ecole de l'Air* based at Salon was ordered to create another Polish unit with seven of these aircraft on 16 May. It actually received nine of them. The school itself had its own local defence flight with Dewoitine 520s. At Bourges, the defence flight was equipped with Curtiss Hawks, where ten were in service. They managed to shoot down a number of German aircraft.

Meanwhile, on the front line, small numbers of French aircraft threw themselves at the advancing German ground forces. Little by little, attrition was beginning to make its mark. Between the period 26 May to 3 June 1940 the evacuation of the British Expeditionary Force (BAE) and large numbers of French troops was being undertaken at Dunkirk. The RAF provided much of the air cover for this operation, but Bloch 152s of GCII/8, operating out of Lympne, were also on hand. These aircraft had left France on the afternoon of 30 May and had been ordered to support the 1st French Army, which by this time had been surrounded. There was a delay in being able to deploy them, as the engine oil designed for Hurricanes did not meet the Bloch 152s requirements. Oil did not arrive until 31 May. Also at Lympne were some Potez 63s belonging to GRI/14 and a pair of Glenn Martin 167s of GBI/63.

The Belgian army had surrendered on 28 May and on 31 May one of the Potez aircraft, escorted by Hurricanes, undertook a reconnaissance mission. Another Potez took off in the afternoon of 1 June, protected by eight Bloch 152s and Hurricanes. The mission was to spot German artillery positions so that the French artillery could zero in on the target. The aircraft arrived just as the Germans were launching a bombing attack against Dunkirk. The Bloch fighters shot down a He111, but then they were nearly attacked themselves by Hurricanes and French anti-aircraft batteries. Once the Dunkirk withdrawal had come to an end GRI/14 and GCII/8 returned to France.

The heaviest fighting had been taking place around the Somme. The French had lost 112 aircraft up to 25 May.

By the beginning of June the *Luftwaffe* was hitting French cities, raiding Marseilles on 1 June and Lyons on 2 June. On the following day, Polish pilots belonging to GCI/145 and flying Caudron Cr714s had their first taste of action. The unit was at Villacoublay, but by this time it had been ordered to Dreux to help defend Paris. Nominally they had thirty-four aircraft, but only eighteen were serviceable.

The *Luftwaffe* struck Paris on 3 June and not only was this Polish unit involved in the interception, but also elements of a number of other units. The alert was sounded at around 1306 hours. An estimated 200 German bombers were inbound, escorted by Bf110s for close support and Bf109s for cover. The Polish-manned aircraft intercepted at around 1310 hours. This was at about the same time as seventeen Dewoitine 520s of GCI/3, out of Meaux, also made contact. The Poles shot down a pair of Bf109s. The Dewoitines shot down three Do17s and a Bf109 for the loss of two fighters.

More units now joined the swirling air battle, with the French then the Germans then the French again ambushing one another's formations. In total, the Germans lost twenty-six aircraft plus a number of others that were badly damaged. Some twelve French pilots lost their lives. On the ground the Germans had hit motor car plants, other factories, railway junctions, and the airfields at Le Bourget and Orly. This was just a taste of what was to come, as on the ground the Germans were about to launch a major attack around the River Aisne.

Significantly, Colonel Charles de Gaulle had been appointed the commander of the new 4th Armoured Division, with a strength of 5,000 men and eighty-five tanks. He would spearhead the counter-attack. De Gaulle would later play a confusing role in the Allies' struggle with Vichy France.

Over the next few days the French Air Force did their utmost to support the ground effort. In the period from 10 May to the morning of 5 June 1940 the French had lost 473 fighters, 194 reconnaissance and observation aircraft and 120 bombers. In comparison, French fighters had had over 375 confirmed kills out of a claimed total of 550.

On 5 June the German preceded their ground attacks with a series of air strikes, coming in at around 0400 hours and primarily aimed at French aircraft on the ground. At this point the French could deploy three fighter and six bomber squadrons.

Three whole German panzer corps manoeuvred to attack across the River Somme. The French army managed to effectively halt the advancing enemy, having been able to create a number of strong points. But by the evening of 7 June German armoured units, led by Rommel, were just short of the River Seine and Rouen. The halting of the German main force was ably assisted by the French Air Force. Some eighteen Breguet 693 bombers, escorted by Curtiss Hawks, had inflicted great damage to lead units of the German ground forces close to Amiens. The *Luftwaffe* pounced on the bombers and their escorts on the return flight. The Germans, in the ensuing battle, only managed to down one of the Curtiss Hawks for the loss of eight of their own fighters.

There were other attacks that day, notably against German armour near Bray Sur Somme, when eighteen Glenn Martin 167 bombers, protected by twenty-three fighters, attacked.

Over the course of 5 June the French bombers had flown 126 sorties. The counteroffensive continued into the night, with attacks even being made on Frankfurt and Bonn. It was never going to be enough, however, as the French army was ultimately forced to continue its retreat, which meant that the air force had to abandon large numbers of bases. It is believed that some fifteen French fighters were lost over the course of 5 June, but they had claimed some sixty-six German aircraft.

Over the next few days the pilots of GCI/6, GCII/2 and GCIII/7 in Morane 406s valiantly tried to blunt the German armoured attacks using their 20 mm guns. Around thirty-six aircraft were used in these attacks, of which about a dozen were shot down. It was a case of desperate measures for desperate times.

By 12 June the Germans had successfully established three bridge-heads on the lower Seine River. Day by day, more French towns and cities were falling to the Germans. The momentous decision to abandon Paris was made on 13 June. For the French Air Force, the hundred or so fighters that had been detailed to protect the capital managed to concentrate at Auxerre.

On 11 June Italy had declared war on France and on 13 June a formation of Fiat CR42 biplanes appeared over the airbase at Le Luc, on the French Riviera. The field was the home of GCIII/6, with their Dewoitine 520s. As the Italians appeared, some of the French aircraft had just landed from a patrol, but others were still aloft, including Adjutant Le Gloan. In the ensuing air battle he shot down four Italian Fiat fighters and shot up an Italian bomber. That night French bombers hit targets in Italy.

On 14 June it was decided that the bulk of the French bomber force would be withdrawn to bases in North Africa. Bombers were to make their way south and cross the coast between Marseilles and Marignane. Other units were ordered to fight on and began to assemble at airfields at Salon de Provence and Istres. Altogether, some eleven groups would remain to fight to the very end.

It is believed that the last mission flown against German targets took place on 24 June 1940. The targets were German pontoon bridges. Before that, the French fighters continued to support the army's weakening efforts. Dewoitine 520s of GCIII/3 attacked and shot down several German aircraft in the Auxerre area on 16 June. The following day an order was issued instructing all fighter groups with Dewoitine, Curtiss or Bloch aircraft to leave for North Africa. The day after, Charles de Gaulle made his famous speech, urging the French to continue to fight. By now, de Gaulle was safe in a BBC studio in London. Fighter groups began moving to Algeria. The ground crews were left to fend for themselves and to get on any available ship transport to take them across the Mediterranean.

In the period 20 to 24 June, reconnaissance aircraft made their way to North Africa. The armistice was finally signed on 22 June, but this was not the end of operations. There were still scattered elements of bomber and fighter formations bombing German units near Lyons, Genoa, Grenoble and Chambéry. Morane 406s of GCI/6 hit German armoured units and trucks around Beaurepaire. Second Lieutenant Raphenne was shot down in the attack and killed. This was just four hours before the armistice came into effect. The lieutenant was probably the last member of the French Air Force to be killed in the battle for France. The Germans would later bury him with full military honours.

For all of the problems that the French Air Force had been struggling with in the run up to hostilities, and the appallingly bad showing that the French ground forces had exhibited during the campaign, the French Air Force's record was comparatively good. In all, although the figures can only ever be approximate, the French Air Force lost 1,200 aircraft to all causes. Despite this, the strength of the French Air Force at the end of operations on 25 June 1940 was actually greater than when war was declared in September 1939. In the period from 10 May to 12 June, French industry had delivered 1,131 new aircraft; some 668 of these were fighters. Many of the French aircraft losses during this period had been of older types of aircraft, but all of the replacements were obviously modern ones.

The exodus of French aircraft from the mainland was by no means complete. Large numbers of aircraft, many of which had literally just been delivered, fell into German hands. This included 453 Morane 406s, 170 Dewoitine 520s, 260 Bloch 152s and a host of other aircraft, including Curtiss Hawks and Glenn Martins.

Armistice arrangements meant that a large proportion of France would become an occupied zone. The rump of France, or the non-occupied zone, was centred round the spa town of Vichy. Around three-fifths of France, including all of the Channel and Atlantic ports and Paris, were occupied. The French continued to administer their colonies without any interference from the Germans. In fact, the Germans had no interest in the French colonies in Africa, or, for that matter, the Middle East. What did remain a problem, however, was the French fleet. Like the French Air Force, some of the vessels had made their way to Britain, while the majority had fled to North Africa.

The new head of the Vichy Government was Philippe Pétain. He was a career soldier and by February 1916 had risen to the rank of general. He had taken command of the French 2nd Army at Verdun and, despite crippling casualties, had held it against the Germans, so gaining his reputation. A year later he became commander in chief of the French army. Pétain had ridden a grey charger on Bastille Day, 14 July 1919, at the head of a victory parade in Paris. It was sixteen days after the signing of the Treaty of Versailles, which for many would be one of the prime reasons for the outbreak of the Second World War.

Out of the post armistice chaos of 1940, Pétain emerged as a man that could end an unpopular war. He was determined to secure France's future, perhaps to become Germany's partner rather than another occupied country. France was still powerful. Its air force was still strong and its navy was intact. Although scattered and under armed, hundreds of thousands of French soldiers protected France's colonial possessions. Pétain was as sure as the Germans that it would only be a matter of weeks before Britain was forced to come to terms with Germany. In this certainty, Pétain was determined to preserve what he could of France and to rebuild. He would not risk what remained of the empire on a throw of the dice by continuing to support the cause against German aggression.

So it was that many thousands of Frenchmen found themselves cast adrift from their homeland and ordered to protect and to preserve France until the time came when she could rise again as a true force in Europe.

Chapter Two

Dakar

The *Surcouf*, a huge French submarine, had left Brest harbour at dusk on 18 June 1940. She had dreadful teething problems, and ever since she had been constructed had spent more time being repaired than on manoeuvres. At around dawn on 19 June she had been spotted by an RAF Coastal Command Sunderland flying boat. They exchanged recognition signals and the submarine continued towards the Cornish coast and then up to Plymouth Sound. Here, the crew were ordered to Devonport and berthed alongside the elderly French dreadnought, *Paris*.

It had been an uneasy time for the crew of the submarine and they received a signal just before dawn on 3 July from the new French naval headquarters at Bordeaux. The orders were to scuttle the submarine immediately. But it was too late. The British, concerned that the French Navy would fall into German hands, had begun to take steps to seize as many French vessels as they could. They were already in the process of boarding coastal patrol boats and converted trawlers. Sixty men had been assigned to seize the *Surcouf*. They were a mixture of Royal Marines and sailors from the submarine HMS *Thames*, under the leadership of Commander Denis Lofty Sprague. The men were armed with revolvers and pickaxe handles. The Marines had rifles and bayonets. It was hoped that a show of force would bring about an immediate surrender. Under the cover of darkness a group had already seized *Paris*.

Men began clambering down the gangplank towards the French submarine. Initially, all went well, until the alarm was raised that there were armed British troops on board. The French started destroying equipment and documents as Sprague's men unlocked hatches and began to enter the submarine. The French officers found in the command post refused to surrender unless they received direct orders from French superior officers. Sprague patiently explained to them in French that they had no option. The French officers were still armed and there were a few moments of tense stand-off, until one of the French men opened fire. There was a vicious melee and an exchange of shots. Two of the British were killed and a number of the men were wounded on both sides, including Sprague, who died at the Plymouth Naval Hospital the following day. It was to be just the beginning.

The bulk of the French fleet was in Mediterranean ports, notably at Mers-el-Kébir, some four miles to the west of the commercial port of Oran in French Algeria. There was also another force at Alexandria. The most significant French force lay in anchor near Oran, under the command of Admiral Gensoul.

The Admiral faced a difficult set of choices. According to the armistice agreement, they were effectively to stand down and remain in port. But he was concerned that the Italians might make a move on Algeria and that his naval force would be vital in protecting French interests.

Further to the east was Force X, under Vice Admiral René Godfroy. They were in Alexandria in Egypt and had been operating with Commander-in-Chief, Mediterranean Fleet, Sir Andrew Cunningham's Royal Naval Mediterranean Fleet. Even when the armistice had been about to take effect, Force X had been involved in raids on Italian shipping around Sicily. The force consisted of a battleship, three heavy cruisers, a light cruiser, three destroyers and a submarine. Godfroy and Cunningham got on extremely well. The Frenchman had been ordered to make for French Tunisia. Cunningham had been ordered to stop him from doing this. Both disregarding their orders, they came to a gentleman's agreement; providing the French agreed not to sail, Cunningham would take no further action.

On 24 June 1940 Admiral Sir Dudley North, who commanded the Royal Navy's North Atlantic station, based in Gibraltar, had arrived on board HMS *Douglas* to speak to Gensoul at Mers-el-Kébir. It was a difficult conversation; technically speaking, the French were now neutral. North tried to convince Gensoul that he should sail his vessels to Britain. Gensoul reassured North that under no circumstances would his French fleet fall into German or Italian hands. Under no circumstances would he leave harbour and join up with the Royal Navy. It was clear, even after North had left, that the British were still more than concerned about the powerful fleet sitting at Mers-el-Kébir. Reconnaissance seaplanes out of Gibraltar buzzed the vessels.

The British tried again; this time Captain Hooky Holland, the captain of HMS *Ark Royal*, arrived at Mers-el-Kébir on board HMS *Foxhound*. The British had put into effect Operation *Catapult* and to this end Force H, under Admiral Sir James Fownes Somerville, had set out from Gibraltar. Somerville's orders were explicit; he was to tell Gensoul that Britain would never surrender and that under no circumstances would Britain allow the French Navy to fall into enemy hands. To this end, he could offer Gensoul three options; the first was to join the Royal Navy and fight alongside Britain. The second option was to sail with a skeleton crew to a British port, where the crew would be repatriated and the vessels manned by Royal Navy personnel. The third option he was given was to sail again with a skeleton crew either to the West Indies or the United States, where, effectively, the vessels would be demilitarized. There was a fourth option and a timescale. If Gensoul did not concur with one of the three options then Somerville was under orders to sink the French fleet.

Despite the close friendship between Gensoul and Holland, the French admiral confirmed that he would defend himself if attacked. Reluctantly, the French were then given the ultimatum and they had until 1500 hours. Already, Swordfish biplanes from HMS *Ark Royal* had dropped mines into the harbour entrance. It was part of Somerville's attempts to convince the French that he was not bluffing.

The French did, however, appear to be readying themselves to leave port. At 1415 hours HMS *Foxhound* received a message from Gensoul. It told them that he had no intention of putting to sea. He confirmed that he had contacted the French government and was awaiting instructions. He went on to assure them that conflict was not a foregone conclusion.

Somerville sent an immediate reply, requesting that it be passed on to Gensoul. He told the Frenchman that if he was prepared to accept the terms then he was to hoist a large chequered flag on the masthead. If he failed to do so then Somerville would open fire at 1500.

With twenty minutes to spare before the bombardment Somerville received a second message from Gensoul. It told him that the Frenchman was prepared to meet one of Somerville's representatives in person for further discussions.

Holland set off towards Mers-el-Kébir again, with the new deadline of 1730 hours. The French had been using the time to prepare. The coastal batteries had been readied and some forty-two aircraft had been rearmed and were ready to take off. Tugs had been brought up to help move the large French vessels away from the jetty. Buoys had been sunk with machine-gun fire. They had been holding up sections of the steel anti-submarine net.

At around 1615 hours, Holland clambered aboard *Dunkerque*. He could see that the French had prepared themselves and that, where possible, guns had swung round in the direction of the British fleet. When he met Gensoul, the Frenchman made it clear that by firing on his vessels it would be a declaration of war between France and Britain. At the same time, Gensoul tried to reassure Holland that he would scuttle his own vessels if either the Germans or the Italians attempted to seize them. Holland patiently explained that this was not an acceptable guarantee.

The two men continued to argue and to talk. It was now just thirty minutes before the final deadline. While Holland was still onboard, Somerville sent another message to Gensoul. It was another warning. He told him that if none of the British proposals had been accepted by 1730 then he would be left with no choice other than to open fire and sink the French vessels. Holland was allowed to send back the return message to Somerville. It confirmed that the crews onboard the French vessels had been reduced, but if the French fleet was still threatened then they would attempt to make for Martinique or the United States. He went on to say that there seemed little chance that Gensoul would accept anything less.

Holland left the French vessel with five minutes to spare before the deadline. He reached HMS *Foxhound*'s motorboat ten minutes later. They were about a mile out to sea at 1754 hours when the first shots were heard. In the space of the next ten minutes the three battleships under Somerville's command fired thirty-six salvos of 15-inch shells, a total of 288 rounds. Most of the major vessels were straddled with shells, inflicting catastrophic damage and crew casualties. Out of the chaos came *Strasbourg*, *Dunkerque's* sister ship and behind her *Tigre*, an old destroyer. The pair of them was determined to escape.

Gensoul sent a signal to Somerville asking him to ceasefire, and then a second saying that most of his ships were out of action and he was evacuating. Somerville signalled back: 'Unless I see your ship sinking I shall open fire again.'

The French had tried to fire back but had so far achieved very little.

Royal Navy aerial reconnaissance aircraft were aloft, and they quickly relayed the movement of the two French vessels. Also aloft were six Swordfish, along with a fighter escort of three Blackburn Skuas. They were quickly diverted to attack, rather than finish off the crippled French vessels in the port, which had been their original mission. As the Royal Naval aircraft closed they saw a pair of HMS *Ark Royal's* spotter aircraft being attacked by five French Curtiss Hawks. The Skuas tried to intervene, but one of them was shot down by the French fighters. The Curtiss Hawks then tried to chase away the Swordfish, followed by the slower-moving remaining pair of Skuas.

Four French Morane 406s had also arrived and the Skuas were now badly outnumbered. One of the two Skuas was piloted by a former ship's officer and commander of the Skua squadron, Lieutenant Bill Bruen. Bruen and Sub-Lieutenant Guy Brokensha spotted nine French fighters above and behind the Swordfish. This was at around 1910. There was a dogfight, during which Brokensha hit a Curtiss 75, which then broke off. Bruen shot at a Morane that was chasing Brokensha and it too broke off and dived away. The British then engaged other French aircraft; three guns on each of the Skuas jammed during the dogfight, but they still had two working guns. At around 1930 three more French Hawks appeared and there was yet another dogfight. The Swordfish then began their attack and came under fire from the *Strasbourg*. The Skuas then peeled off and headed home, attacking a French flying boat *en route*. The French aircraft was dropping bombs on a British destroyer. Brokensha managed to knock out one of the flying boat's engines and the Skuas then returned to the *Ark Royal* and landed just after sunset.

As it was, the Swordfish attack on the *Strasbourg* was a failure and the French vessel managed to shoot down two of the Swordfish with its anti-aircraft guns. The six aircrew were later picked up by the destroyer HMS *Wrestler*.

More of the French vessels were trying to escape the trap and were now engaging Somerville's fleet. HMS *Ark Royal*'s Swordfish were sent up again in the fading light. This time they were armed with torpedoes and would have to come in low against very accurate anti-aircraft fire. Fortunately, however, French ships lacked radar, so it was possible for four of the Swordfish to let their torpedoes go before the last two were spotted and came under fire. Once again, the attack was inconclusive and with sunset at 2035 hours it was the end of all possible offensive actions for the day.

Two submarines, HMS *Pandora* and HMS *Proteus*, were left to prowl the waters, hoping to find targets. Meanwhile, feverish preparations were underway on HMS *Ark Royal* to prepare all available aircraft for another attack at first light. The aircraft carrier could muster twelve Swordfish and nine Skuas. The day's casualties, as far as the French were concerned, were 1,297 dead and 350 wounded. The vast majority of casualties had been inflicted when the *Bretagne* had capsized.

The British were adamant that the distasteful engagement had been necessary. Unsurprisingly, the French viewed it as an act of war, yet they were in no position to retaliate beyond diplomatic channels and a token attack on Gibraltar.

The British had played into the hands of the Anglophobes, at the heart of the new Vichy government. The hopelessness of the situation and the possibility that the same action would be taken against Godfroy at Alexandria finally persuaded him to mothball his squadron. An arrangement was made for his crews to be repatriated to Vichy France, unless of course they wanted to continue the fight. Very few chose this option.

A similar situation faced Pierre Boisson, the Governor General of French West Africa, at Dakar, and the local naval commander,

Admiral Placon. They had been approached by Acting Rear Admiral Rodney Onslow on 7 July 1940. They were offered exactly the same terms that Somerville had offered Gensoul. In fact, shortly after the ultimatum had been presented, the British intercepted a French signal ordering all vessels in Dakar to 'meet attacks from the English enemy with the utmost ferocity'.

Onslow knew the port of Dakar extremely well; until the armistice had been signed he had been based there with HMS *Hermes* and part of the Anglo-French squadron searching for German commerce raiders in the South Atlantic. Sitting in Dakar harbour was a major threat – the *Richelieu*, with eight 15-inch guns. In the early hours of the morning of 8 July, a black-painted motorboat pulled alongside the French vessel. On board was a nine-man crew, armed to the teeth, but also supplied with four depth charges. Leading the raid was Commander Bobby Bristow.

Bristow's orders were to inflict as much damage to the French battleship as possible, ideally crippling her for a year. Bristow man-oeuvred the motorboat to the stern of the French battleship. They then heaved the four depth charges over the side, hoping that the explosions would wreck the propellers and flood the compartments in the stern.

The tides were against Bristow and the depth charges sank to the bottom in insufficient water. Certain that they had failed, Bristow ordered the motorboat out of the harbour. By 0400 hours, he had told Onslow that the raid had not worked. Consequently, Onslow had to quickly improvise and six Swordfish took off in darkness, at 0415 hours, from the deck of HMS *Hermes*.

At first they reported that four of the torpedoes dropped by the Swordfish had been seen running towards the battleship. In fact, only one had struck the vessel, but it had also detonated the depth charges. A vast hole was torn into the French battleship's hull. Her stern began to sink into the silt and her compartments were flooded.

Although the French battleship had not been destroyed, it had certainly been put out of action and Dakar was entirely unable to provide the machinery and equipment that would be needed to make the necessary repairs. However, although the *Richelieu* was immobile, she would serve as a major thorn in the British side, and that of de Gaulle, before the year was out.

The British attacks and threats had only served to reinforce the French position with the Germans and the Italians to allow them to rearm. Consequently, GCI/3, GCII/3, GCIII/3, GCIII/6 and GCII/7 had some 165 Dewoitine D520s. Five other units were issued with 146 Curtiss Hawks, including GCI/5 and GCII/5 in Morocco. Four more groups were equipped with Morane 406s in both Syria and North Africa. This meant that there were around 200 French fighters. There was also a small detachment, EC2/565 on Madagascar. Around 200 French bombers were available, the majority of them in North Africa. GBI/39 was in Syria, GBI/62 and GBI/63 were in Mali, and GBII/62 and GBII/63 were in Senegal. Four groups were equipped with Douglas DB7s, including GBI/19 and GBI/32. Other, older aircraft, were also still in service. There was even a small squadron of Farman 222s in Indochina and an independent group in Senegal. In the Lebanon there were Bloch 200 bombers. Reconnaissance units were based on airfields as widely scattered as Algeria, Morocco, and Syria.

In unoccupied France there were several units with Bloch 152s and Bloch 155s, each with a strength of twenty-four aircraft. Night fighter units were also operational, using Potez 631s. There were a number of fighter groups also in the south-east and south-west of France and two additional fighter groups, GCI/1 and GCII/9, in reserve at Lyons and Aulnat.

The Germans allowed the French aircraft industry to continue to produce aircraft for unoccupied France. In the occupied zone the French aircraft industry was ordered to gear up to produce German aircraft for the *Luftwaffe*. Amongst the aircraft being built were Dewoitine 520s at Toulouse.

The British attacks had done nothing to help de Gaulle's cause in trying to convince any able-bodied Frenchman to join his crusade to liberate France with a Free French, all services force. There were many thousands of French men who had to be repatriated to France as a result.

On 24 July 1940 a French steamer, *Meknes*, had been stopped by a German motor torpedo boat off Portland. It had then torpedoed the steamer. On board were 1,277 French sailors. British destroyers rushed to the scene and rescued around 900 of them, but upwards of 400 were drowned, including the crew of the vessel.

Towards the end of July a handful of Free French aircrew were involved on a bombing raid on the Ruhr, partially crewing RAF Bomber Command aircraft. De Gaulle was able to announce that France was still in the war against Germany.

In response to the attack against the French fleet at Mers-el-Kébir the Vichy Government had launched a bombing raid against Gibraltar on 18 July 1940. It was a half-hearted attack and the majority of the bombs were deliberately dropped short of their targets.

On 20 September 1940, in plain clothes and accompanied by two other officers, Commandant Hettier de Boislambert, a Free French officer, was heading for Dakar. His mission was to recruit as many Vichy officers to the Free French cause as possible. He was to pave the way for an Anglo-French attempt on Dakar, codenamed Operation *Menace*. The officer was convinced that it would only take a word for the leading officers of the Dakar garrison to defect. Reality could not have been further from the truth. Vichy had over 100,000 troops across Algeria, Morocco and Tunisia. Although many of them were colonial troops, they would follow the lead of their officers.

There was already a tension developing between de Gaulle and Churchill. This would ultimately mean that the French would be kept out of many of the key decisions when the three great powers, Britain, the United States and the Soviet Union, began to discuss and implement strategic objectives for the conduct of the war. De Gaulle was obviously keen to make a contribution and to show that the French opinion and priorities still mattered. Back in June 1940 he had said during a radio broadcast: 'Remember this, France does not stand alone. Behind her stands a vast empire.'

Against Churchill's better judgement he had brought de Gaulle into the planning and preparation for Operation *Menace*. It was to be a supreme mistake, as the whole operation became a topic of conversation in the clubs in London.

De Gaulle was determined to put a positive spin on the whole operation. He predicted that an immense fleet of 100 or more vessels would appear at dawn and slowly approach Dakar. The fleet would send friendship messages to the town, to the garrison and to the French navy. Amongst the fleet there would be Frenchmen, along with the British, Dutch, Poles and Belgians. A small ship would approach with a white flag and the envoys of de Gaulle himself would meet with the governor. They would try to convince him that they came in peace and wanted cooperation, but if Dakar chose to resist then they would be crushed. Free French and British aircraft would be dropping leaflets over Dakar and on the streets there would be discussions about the advantages of a battle being avoided. De Gaulle hoped that the governor would feel that if he resisted then it would be for nothing and that, perhaps, he would, for his own honour, fire a few shots at the allied fleet. But that would be sufficient. By evening the governor and representatives of the allied fleet would dine together and drink towards a final allied victory.

The fleet that appeared off Dakar around dawn on 23 September 1940 was impressive. The centre point was HMS *Ark Royal*. The troops designated to land included 2,400 French; the rest of them comprised a brigade of Royal Marines, over 4,000 of them. The infantry were spread over four liners, which indicates the impromptu nature of the whole expedition.

It was hoped that the Dakar expedition would be bloodless and even Churchill was having second thoughts. Churchill was actually thinking that the whole operation should be abandoned. There was a way of avoiding any potential loss of prestige and still keeping the purpose of the concentration of the vessels a secret. Churchill thought that the whole expedition could be diverted to Douala and could then cover de Gaulle's operations in the French Cameroons. After that the vessels could then disperse and return to their home ports.

It should have been fairly clear that this was not going to be bloodless and neither did de Gaulle have a great deal of support. A prime example was the interception of a French coaster based at Dakar, *Poitiers*. It was intercepted by HMS *Cumberland*. Rather than allow the ship to fall into British hands, they had opened the seacocks and set fire to the deck cargo. They then promptly abandoned ship, shouting their support for both Pétain and for Hitler.

At dawn on 23 September a pair of unarmed Caudron C272 Luciole liaison aircraft took off from HMS *Ark Royal*. They were bound for the fighter base on the Cape Verde peninsula. The Free

French crews landed and laid out a canvas signal panel, indicating to a Swordfish flying above that the next phase of the operation could be mounted. Three Free French officers were landed by the Swordfish. As the Swordfish flew off again it was intercepted by a Curtiss Hawk, which opened fire on it.

Meanwhile, other Swordfish had been dropping leaflets over the town and the harbour. The anti-aircraft guns on the *Richelieu* opened fire on them at 0610 hours. Also, the French crews of the Lucioles, along with the three French officers, had all been taken prisoner. On one of the prisoners they found a list of Free French sympathisers. They were all quickly rounded up.

A Free French motor launch was sent to see how the situation was developing. The Frenchmen on board were told in no uncertain terms that Dakar was prepared to defend itself and that in no way did it support de Gaulle. Soon afterwards, the Anglo-French fleet began to come under fire from the coastal guns. Reluctantly, the British began firing back, targeting the *Richelieu* and the forts containing the coastal guns. Both the British and the French were firing blind as there was thick fog and no opportunity for aerial spotter planes.

The Vichy French got in the first major damage, hitting HMS *Cumberland.* The destroyer HMS *Foresight* was also hit. The British retaliated by hitting a Vichy French submarine and a French merchant ship was also hit in the port of Dakar. It was clear that Dakar was not about to surrender, so, instead, a proportion of the British fleet sailed thirteen miles east of Dakar, to Rufisque Bay, where 180 French Marines would be landed.

Vichy French spotter aircraft noticed them and the super destroyer *L'Audacieux*, was sent out to investigate. Following her were three other vessels, *Georges Leygues, Montcalm* and *Le Malin.* Lagging far behind was the Vichy sloop *Surprise.*

The largest British vessel was HMAS *Australia*, a heavy cruiser. She had with her a pair of destroyers, HMS *Fury* and HMS *Greyhound.* The Australian sailors on board HMAS *Australia* had never fired their main armaments in anger before. Nonetheless, they opened fire on the Vichy vessels with vengeance. They wrecked the bridge of *L'Audacieux*, killing eighty-one of the crew. The ship was ablaze and drifting towards the shore. When one of the British destroyers tried to pick up survivors the Vichy French coastal batteries opened up on her. The sloop, *Surprise*, managed to save just 186 of the crewmen.

Swordfish from HMS *Ark Royal* had spotted the Vichy ships making for Rufisque Bay. But due to the foggy conditions there was little that they could do to lend a hand.

As the Free French Marines approached the coastline they came under fire from machine guns and a mountain gun. De Gaulle promptly ordered the Marines to withdraw.

All that could now be achieved was another attempt at a bluff. An ultimatum was sent to Governor Boisson and it would expire at 0600 hours on the following day. It read: 'Desiring Frenchmen not to fight against Frenchmen in a pitched battle General de Gaulle has withdrawn his forces.'

The message went on to warn that if an agreement was not made so that the Free French could land then the Royal Navy would open fire. It went further: 'Once fire has begun it will continue until the fortifications of Dakar are entirely destroyed and the place occupied by troops who are ready to fulfil their duty.'

Boisson instructed the signallers on board *Richelieu* to reply: 'France has entrusted me Dakar. I shall defend Dakar to the end.'

There was now nothing for it but to go ahead with the threat. Just after first light six Skuas, each carrying 500 lb armour-piercing bombs, left the deck of the *Ark Royal* in thick fog to attack the *Richelieu* and other French vessels in the harbour. The attack was disappointing, but there had been little anti-aircraft fire and no sign of Vichy aircraft. Another half a dozen aircraft, Swordfish, were launched against the coastal guns in Fort Manual. This was around thirty minutes later and they claimed six hits, but did no real damage to the battery. Another six Swordfish were launched against the same target. Each of these had 250 lb bombs on board. As they were just about to launch they read a message on a blackboard, which said 'change target to *Richelieu*'.

The six pilots acknowledged just as the carrier turned into the wind. As they got aloft they split into two groups, each of three aircraft. The Swordfish took up position to dive bomb the *Richelieu* and almost immediately one of the aircraft was hit by anti-aircraft fire. It plummeted down in flames. The Swordfish then came under attack from three or four Curtiss Hawks. The Swordfish crews took evasive action and began firing. The faster Hawks managed to get on the tails of some of the Swordfish and began to engage. Taking evasive action, the Swordfish had a momentary advantage as the faster French aircraft struggled to turn to continue to engage. Another of the Swordfish was shot down and in the confusion the Swordfish jettisoned their bombs prematurely then struggled to get back to the *Ark Royal*. Initially it was believed that three of the Swordfish had been shot down, with the pilots reporting that at least two had been hit with another possible loss. The Swordfish pilots could not believe that what they had thought to be French allies flying American aircraft had in fact been so determined to kill them. In fact, four of the nine Swordfish aircrew had been killed in this attack. The chances of the Swordfish's bombs even penetrating the 8-inch armour of the *Richelieu* were slim.

There was another aerial engagement, when in the afternoon nine Swordfish and three Skuas set off to find the Vichy vessels hunting for the Free French forces. Two of the Swordfish were lost to anti-aircraft fire.

It was very difficult to know whether or not the Anglo-French fleet was causing any damage, and every time a British aircraft ventured to direct fire or to carry out reconnaissance they were attacked by Curtiss Hawks. There was now the danger that the Vichy French would penetrate the air cover and anti-aircraft screens and bring the British fleet under fire. They had tried on several occasions and there had been near misses. On the same afternoon Vichy bombers, operating out of Morocco, had dropped 150 bombs on Gibraltar. The dockyards were hit, but most of the bombs once again fell into the sea.

It was now abundantly clear that Operation *Menace* had been a fiasco. All that could now be achieved was to blockade Dakar. But given the problems facing the Royal Navy in the Atlantic and in the Mediterranean, there was little chance that they could afford to commit vessels for an unspecified period of time off the West African coast. The pretence at still aiming to overcome Dakar continued for another day. The problem now was that there were clear skies and the chances were that the French gunners would be able to zero in on the British vessels.

There were more aerial combats that day, with the Curtiss Hawks easily outgunning the Swordfish and the Skuas. There was also another raid on Gibraltar, and this time several civilians had been killed and an armed trawler sunk. Through the French naval attaché in Madrid it was made clear that as long as attacks were made on Dakar then the Vichy Air Force would strike Gibraltar.

Reluctantly, the British withdrew from Dakar and the Vichy Government was able to turn it into a stunning victory. After all, their guns had been outnumbered by around eight to one, but they had still prevailed.

Chapter Three

Iraq

An isolated outpost of the French empire was nestled between Eritrea, Ethiopia and British Somaliland, at the junction of the Red Sea and the Gulf of Aden. French Somaliland found itself in an incredibly difficult situation when the hostilities in France were drawing to a close in June 1940.

The Italians were the major aggressors in this theatre of the war. They had considerable ground forces and an extensive range of aircraft. The local French commander, General Legentilhomme, informed British authorities around 18 June that he intended to continue resistance. Already, the Italians had made aggressive moves against Kenya in the south, out of Ethiopia and Italian Somaliland, and certainly had sufficient forces to threaten both British and French Somaliland.

A number of Italian aircraft mounted sorties over French Somaliland out of Dessie in Ethiopia. They struck the French Somaliland capital, Djibouti. They attacked in three waves. The French put up considerable anti-aircraft fire in response on 21 June. On the following day the Italians once again concentrated on Djibouti, bombing the port during the night and then sending in additional waves to attack Djibouti airfield. The probable reason for the attacks was to prevent British aircraft from using Djibouti as a forward base. With the signing of the armistice between Italy and France, operations against Djibouti were suspended on 24 June 1940.

On 28 June the Italians contacted Legentilhomme and requested that he implement the armistice, which would allow the Italians to use the Djibouti to Addis Ababa railway. The Frenchman declined.

By March 1941 the scales had tipped in favour of the British and Commonwealth troops in East Africa. It was now the Italians that found themselves under attack on every front. So far, French

Somaliland had largely kept itself out of the conflict. They were trapped in a situation where they could not be openly hostile to either the British or to the Italians. They were simply able to defend themselves.

One such incident took place on 24 March 1941. The Italian 70th Colonial Division was retreating from Berbera, the capital of British Somaliland. It was suggested that the railway that ran between the frontier of French Somaliland and Dire Dawa should be attacked. Fairey Battles, operating out of Dogabur, dive bombed and destroyed several bridges on the Djibouti section of the line. Vichy French troops opened fire on the aircraft and one of the Battles was hit twenty-two times.

In the period up to the beginning of October 1941, it had proved incredibly difficult to patrol the French Somaliland border. On 2 October three Ju86s belonging to 35 South African Air Force Flight were moved into the area, followed by four Vincents belonging to No. 8 Squadron of the RAF in Aden. On 4 October an Italian S75 was spotted at Djibouti. It was destroyed on the ground on 5 October, which led to strong complaints from the French.

By November the Italians had been soundly beaten and Ethiopia had been conquered. All that now remained was French Somaliland. It was originally suggested that it should be invaded. The only known combat between Vichy aircraft based in French Somaliland and British or Commonwealth forces took place on 11 December 1941. By this time it had been decided only to blockade French Somaliland and force them to allow the British to use the railway from Djibouti. Lieutenant Gazzard, of B Flight belonging to 3 SAAF Squadron, had taken off on a patrol in a Mohawk. He spotted a Potez 631 over the airfield at Djibouti. He chased the Vichy aircraft and the Potez's rear gunner opened fire. Gazzard returned fire and saw smoke pouring out of the port engine of the Potez, but it then escaped into cloud.

The Vichy French continued to hold the colony for just over a year. In December 1942, following a 101-day British blockade, French Somaliland surrendered and Allied forces occupied the colony. It was clear that they were not wholly supporters of the Vichy regime, as a local battalion from French Somaliland was actually deployed in the campaign to liberate France in 1944. France had also been indirectly involved in another conflict in May 1941. Out of the ashes of the Ottoman Empire and the breaking up of its colonies after its defeat in the First World War was the Arab state of Iraq. It was placed under a British mandate until December 1927. Iraq was recognized as an independent state shortly afterwards, and in October 1932 had joined the League of Nations. The treaty, which had been signed between Britain and Iraq, guaranteed the passage of British troops through Iraq in the event of war. It also guaranteed that a British military mission remained attached to the Iraqi army and that two RAF bases would also remain. The first was based at Shaibah, near Basra, in southern Iraq on the Persian Gulf. The other was on the Euphrates River, close to a large lake called Habbaniya, earning the base its name. This airbase was situated on the main Baghdad to Haifa road, just over fifty miles to the west of Baghdad.

The closest French airbase was some 300 miles to the east at Palmyra in Syria. The location of this French airfield was to cause considerable problems. Strategically speaking, both of the RAF bases were incredibly important to the British. In effect, they linked the land route between India and Egypt. The majority of the troops were Christian members of the Assyrian constabulary.

At Habbaniya, these men, supported by a handful of RAF armoured cars, patrolled a seven-mile long perimeter. The base operated as the advance training facility, 4 Service Flying Training School. The base itself was highly vulnerable, as it lay in low ground and was overlooked by a high plateau. The writing should have been on the wall at the outbreak of the war in 1939. The Iraqis, only after significant pressure, broke off diplomatic relations with Germany. They never declared war and neither did they break off relations with Italy. As a consequence, Iraq became the centre of anti-British feeling across the whole region.

Haj Amin al-Husseini, the Grand Mufti of Jerusalem, had been given sanctuary in Baghdad following his failed Palestinian rebellion, which came to an end in 1939. In January 1941 the pro-Axis prime minister of Iraq, Rashid Ali al-Gaylani, was forced out of power. But after Greece and Libya had fallen to the Germans, four Iraqi colonels, known as the Golden Square, staged a coup and restored Rashid Ali. At the time King Faisal II of Iraq was a five-year-old and living in Kurdistan.

Fortuitously, two British Indian army brigades that had been earmarked for Singapore were still at Karachi. Instead, they were sent to Basra. An additional 400 men belonging to the King's Own Royal Regiment were also flown in. Arguably, this was the first time that the British army airlifted whole units into a theatre. They were using Vickers Valentia biplanes. Understandably, Rashid Ali was not altogether pleased with the arrival and, in fact, when the second brigade disembarked at Basra they were sniped at by a mob led by Iraqi police.

Even though the British had reinforced Iraq they were still hopelessly outnumbered. Each of the brigades that they had sent was about 5,000 strong, but this was against an Iraqi army in excess of 60,000. Behind the scenes the Italians and Germans agreed to back Rashid Ali and the colonels and to provide them with thirty-three aircraft. The shipment would include fourteen Bf110s, seven He111s and twenty transport aircraft. Italy would contribute by sending twelve CR42s. It was at this point that Vichy France stepped in to help facilitate this agreement. There would have been little chance of the Germans or the Italians making good their pledges, which also included small arms and cash.

Admiral Darlan had become a key member of the Vichy regime. In effect, he was Pétain's deputy; he was Minister for the Interior, Defence and Foreign Affairs. Darlan was fully supportive of agreements with the Germans in order to promote long-term French aims. The agreement between the Iraqis, the Germans and the Italians came at a time when Darlan was at the height of his powers and, effectively, the head of the Vichy government, with Pétain as a willing figurehead.

The proposal was that access to Iraq would be facilitated via French-held Syria. Darlan was determined to make the British pay. As had been the case in every conflict that the French had found themselves in when opposing Britain, the Royal Navy was their greatest foe. The Royal Navy had tightened the blockade on colonial imports into Marseilles, including shipments of rubber from Indochina.

Sometimes, when prosecuting Operation *Ration*, as the British called it, they had been brought into direct conflict with Vichy French military forces. On one particular occasion, just off

Casablanca, HMS *Sheffield* had got into a fire fight with the French shore battery. After several volleys HMS *Sheffield* had hit a magazine and there was a massive explosion. The Vichy French responded with an attack by ten Glenn Martin bombers. They managed to catch up with HMS *Sheffield* and a number of British destroyers just outside Gibraltar. However, they failed to inflict any damage on the cruiser.

There had been other incidents and Darlan had had his men calculate that since July 1940 the British had seized no fewer than 167 ships. In Darlan's mind the British were nothing other than pirates. All of this served to rile the French and as a result they were more than happy to open their airfields for Axis use. Darlan was happy to come to agreement with the Germans in order to combat France's long-term foe. He began negotiations to offer the Germans a submarine base at Dakar and also offered the use of Bizerte, in Tunisia, so that the sea leg of the supply column from mainland Europe to North Africa would be less hazardous for Rommel's Afrika Korps. At that time the main German receiving port for supplies and equipment was Tripoli and their supply ships were constantly under attack, primarily from British forces based in Malta.

The Germans were quick to seize this opportunity. They released 7,000 French prisoners of war, many of them being professional officers and non-commissioned officers. They also reduced the payments that France had to make each day for the German occupation. The Germans had been charging 20,000,000 Reichsmarks as an occupation levy every day. This was now reduced to 15,000,000 Reichsmarks.

There was also an agreement in place concerning Syria. The document, known as the Paris Protocols, was negotiated by Darlan and the German Ambassador to France, Otto Abetz. It was fully negotiated, but never ratified. Of particular significance was the negotiated agreement about Syria. Darlan proposed that France would launch an offensive against the British-held Iraqi oilfields and that the oil would be made available to the Germans. Unbeknown to the French, a previous agreement with Germany had already been reached with Iraq and Syria to expel the French.

35

This was against a backdrop of a very tricky period for Britain. Lieutenant-General Sir Maitland Wilson had taken a force from North Africa, stripping the British of vitally needed men, on a disastrous expedition to mainland Greece. It had ended in abject failure in April 1941. Only a month before this Rommel had launched an offensive in North Africa and had pushed back what remained of the British forces in North Africa all the way to the Egyptian border. Only Tobruk remained a thorn in Rommel's side. Added to this, there were still requirements in Ethiopia and Somaliland and then came the fiasco of Crete, which led to another close run but humiliating defeat for the British.

In overall charge of British operations in North Africa was General Archibald Wavell. He knew that, sooner or later, Churchill would ask him to make preparations to throw the Vichy French out of Syria and hand it over to de Gaulle. It was a difficult place for the Vichy to protect; the coastal approaches were controlled by the Royal Navy, primarily operating out of Cyprus. Britain controlled Palestine, Transjordan and, until the problems with Rashid Ali, Iraq. This, effectively, meant that the south and the east of Syria were British controlled. The Vichy could expect no assistance from neutral Turkey to the north. There were already talks about de Gaulle's Free French getting involved. It was the Free French contention that with a show of force, along with the 6,000 Gaullist troops promised, the Vichy regime in Syria could be toppled with the minimum of effort.

There was a series of increasingly terse telegrams between Churchill and Wavell in mid-1941. Wavell was insistent that it was foolhardy to become involved in either Iraq or Palestine. Churchill, on the other hand, recognized the importance of the oilfields to the war effort. Wavell tried to counsel caution and carefully tried to point out that by getting involved in Iraq or Palestine the defence of Egypt would be compromised. Broadly speaking, the British chiefs of staff were in agreement with Wavell, but, ultimately, Churchill persuaded them to back down. They would take offensive action in Iraq and they would consider the options open to them to deal with Syria.

By 1 May 1941 around 9,000 Iraqi troops, supported by fifty guns, were surrounding Habbaniya airfield. The British had converted sixty Hawker Audaxes and Airspeed Oxfords so that they could carry bombs. The available crews had been trained as best as possible. There were also a number of Greek pilots, many of whom could not speak English and had never flown on an operation. The British, however, had begun building up at Basra. Vickers Wellington bombers of 70 Squadron had already arrived.

Theoretically, the Iraqi Air Force was far bigger than anything that the RAF could bring together. They had twenty-five airworthy Hawker Nisrs, which were effectively Audaxes with Pegasus engines, at Mosul. This was designated 1 (Army Cooperation) Squadron. At Kirkuk was 4 (Fighter) Squadron, with nine airworthy Gloster Gladiators. At Rashid, Baghdad, was 5 (Fighter) Squadron, with fifteen Italian Breda Ba65 attack aircraft and 7 (Fighter Bomber) Squadron with fifteen Douglas-Northrop 8A-4 attack bombers. Also at Rashid were four Italian Savoia SM79B bombers. There were also other aircraft available, including de Havilland Dragons, Avro Ansons and Tiger Moths.

The Iraqis were given an ultimatum to withdraw their forces around the airbase by 1 May 1941. When they refused, the British were resolved to attack the Iraqis at dawn on 2 May, without any further negotiation. Meanwhile, trenches were being built all around the perimeter of Habbaniya in order to improve the defences.

The first British attack came in against the Iraqi forces around the airbase, from the Wellingtons at Basra. They made a low-level, daybreak attack. Only one of the Wellingtons failed to get back to Basra. Both of its engines were knocked out even before it had been able to drop its bombs, but it landed safely on Habbaniya airfield, where it came under immediate fire from the Iraqi artillery.

Meanwhile, aircraft were scrambled from the airfield itself. They bombed and strafed the Iraqi positions. The attack force, consisting of around thirty-five aircraft, could attack, land at the airfield, be refuelled and rearmed and be back in the air in ten minutes. In command of this force was Squadron Leader Tony Dudgeon. Dudgeon knew that time was not on their side and that they needed to destroy as many Iraqi weapons and vehicles as they could before they could be brought to bear on the base. The British had to harry the Iraqis and fly as many missions as possible, with any aircraft that were available to them. Consequently, the aircraft were sent out to bomb and machinegun and hunt for targets. The determination of the pilots was such that as soon as they had landed one of them would rush to the operations room, report the mission results and then suggest new targets. These would then be plotted onto a photo map for the next mission. While one of the crewmen performed this task the other, with whatever additional assistance he could get, would reload the aircraft and prepare it for takeoff.

By the end of the day the aircraft operating out of the airfield had flown 193 sorties. Four of their aircraft had been destroyed on the ground; two had been shot down with the loss of four crewmen. However, the attacks had inflicted heavy damage on the Iraqi besieging force. What was particularly dangerous was not necessarily the anti-aircraft guns, but the fire from Iraqi infantry machine guns and rifles. The British aircraft were coming in low and were slow moving. This led to a number of crewmen being wounded through the thighs and buttocks, when bullets smashed straight through their seats.

The British persisted, attacking at night to deprive the enemy of sleep. Gradually, Iraqi morale was worn away. So far, the highly trumpeted promise of German aerial support had failed to materialize. It was, however, on its way.

Also on its way, was a hastily thrown together relief column, which was codenamed *Habforce*. It would consist of two columns, one under Brigadier James Kingstone, codenamed *Kingcol*, and the second main column under Lieutenant-Colonel J.S. Nichols. In addition to this were three mechanized squadrons using converted civilian Ford trucks and home-made armoured cars. This was the Arab Legion, commanded by John Bagot Glubb. He had already had a colourful career. He had been commissioned in the Royal Engineers in 1915, was wounded on the Western Front and transferred to Iraq in 1920. He became an officer in the Arab Legion, which was the regular army of Transjordan. Glubb created the desert patrol, which was entirely manned by Bedouins. Glubb had taken over from Frederick Peake as commander of the Arab Legion in 1939.

The Vichy were as good as their word to the Germans. Between 10 and 15 May 1941 German aircraft began arriving in Mosul via the French airbases in Syria. The first German aircraft to actually arrive made for Baghdad on 11 May. It was an He111 and on board was Dr Fritz Grobba, Germany's Ambassador to Iraq, and the newly appointed head of the German military mission to Iraq, Major Axel von Blomberg. As their plane approached Baghdad it came under machine-gun fire, believed to be from Iraqi tribesmen positions. The aircraft made a safe landing at Baghdad airport, but von Blomberg had been shot through the neck and was dead.

By 12 May the immediate threat to Habbaniya had receded and the British withdrew the Wellingtons to Egypt. But on the very same day the first German aircraft were spotted in Iraq; a small contingent, under the command of *Oberst* Werner Junck, had arrived.

The *Luftwaffe* mission to Iraq was variously known as *Sonderkommando Junck*, or by Junck's title, which was rather grandly *Fliegerführer Irak*. It consisted of twelve Bf110s led by *Oberleutnant* Hobein. This force, 4/ZG76, was not the only aircraft group. There were also two Bf110s led by *Leutnant* Woerner of ZG26 and seven He111s of 4/KG4, commanded by *Hauptmann* Schwanhäuser. Five more He111s had left Italy on 12 May and arrived in Syria later the same day. To back up the force there were twenty Ju52 transporters under *Hauptmann* Rother, a 20 mm flak battery and a handful of Ju90 four-engine transports. All of these had left Greek airfields and had been over-painted with Iraqi insignia.

It was an incredibly complex operation and it would have been impossible without the connivance of the Vichy French. Comparatively speaking, all of the aircraft had relatively short ranges. The transports were there to ensure that engineers, bombs, spare parts, tools and a host of other resources were available. As soon as the aircraft were established, the bulk of the Ju52s would have to be relinquished, as they were going to be needed for the German air drop on Crete.

The Germans had not forgotten anything. There was even a flying laboratory, which would test Iraqi fuel and then refine it so that it could be used for the German aircraft. Another of the transports was a communication centre. Inside this were transmitters that would allow Junck to communicate not only with the other airfields in Iraq, but also *Luftwaffe* headquarters in Athens and Berlin. The two main airfields that the Germans would be using would be Rashid and Mosul.

For the RAF, Vichy territory was still off limits, but they had to do something in order to try to intercept the incoming German aircraft. In fact, the first contact with Germans in the area did not take place over Syria but instead over Mosul, on 13 May 1941. A Blenheim fighter of 203 Squadron was on a reconnaissance mission. The aircraft was being piloted by Flying Officer Lane-Sansom when it came under attack four times by a Bf110, which belonged to 4/ZG76. The sighting was confirmed later in the day when Flight Lieutenant Plinston of 84 Squadron bombed the railway near Mosul. He, too, saw a Bf110. It was a confirmation of the RAF's worst fears; the Germans had, in fact, arrived.

Consequently, at 0615 hours on 14 May Pilot Officer Watson of 203 Squadron flew a reconnaissance mission over Syria to see if he could find where the German aircraft were being refuelled. He spotted what he believed to be a Ju90 taking off at Palmyra. He returned to base. Later in the day Watson, along with four Blenheims operating out of Habbaniya, escorted by a pair of Curtiss Tomahawks, bombed and strafed Palmyra airfield.

The British force arrived at around 1740 hours. They saw three Ju90s, a Fiat CR42 fighter and two biplanes, believed to be civilian. At least, this is what Watson reported seeing. The Tomahawk pilots believed that they could see four He111s and a Ju52. This confusion still remains to this day, but according to German records of KG4 the attack took place shortly after three He111s had taken off *en route* to Mosul. The Germans noted that two aircraft on the ground were destroyed. The gloves were certainly off. A reconnaissance mission on 15 May over Palmyra airfield showed a burned-out He111, three more damaged He111s and a shot-up Ju52.

A pair of Tomahawks, flown by Flying Officer Aldridge and Pilot Officer C.R. Caldwell, of 250 Squadron, escorted eight Blenheims of 84 Squadron headed towards Damascus to see if they could find more German aircraft. On the ground was a pair of Ju90s, two Ju52s and a He111. Below, but airborne, was a Morane 406. Sea mist began rolling in, but four of the Blenheims managed to bomb Rayak airfield, killing a French officer.

Perhaps what had convinced Churchill to authorize the attacks against German aircraft in Syria and against Vichy French airfields (of which Rayak airfield was one, being a base for French fighter aircraft) was not just the arrival of the *Luftwaffe*. On 13 May, from Syria via Turkey, a train load of supplies had pulled into Mosul. On board the train were 15,500 rifles, 6,000,000 rounds of ammunition, 200 machine guns with 900 belts of ammunition, four 75 mm field guns and 100 rounds; and this would just be the first to arrive.

Vichy French air forces in Syria primarily consisted of GCI/7 with a total strength of twenty-six Morane 406 fighters. There were also Potez 25 aircraft in five *Groupes Aérines de Reconnaissance* (GAO) units. These were based at Aleppo, Baalbek, Deir-ez-Zor, Palmyra and Rayak. Also at Aleppo were more modern Potez 63-IIs.

The war of attrition against the *Luftwaffe* continued. So far, the Vichy French aircraft had chosen for the most part not to intercede, even though their bases were coming under attack and were being continually buzzed and photographed by RAF aircraft. By 18 May *Kingcol* had arrived at Habbaniya, having come under strafing attacks from two or three Bf109s in the final approach.

On the same day, a pair of South African Air Force Marylands was heading towards Syria. The aircraft were flown by Lieutenant Labat and Commandant Goumin. Shortly after midday, Labat's aircraft was chased by four Morane 406s but they failed to catch him. Later, three Blenheims of 84 Squadron were inbound for a raid on Rayak. They were intercepted by three Morane 406s belonging to *Groupe de Chasse* I/7. One of the French pilots, *Sergeant Chef* Veillie, attacked two of the Blenheims. Lieutenant de la Taille and *Sous Lieutenant* Trulla attacked the third bomber. Again, no damage was inflicted.

The Iraqi forces were still coming under tremendous attack, now not just from the RAF but also from ground forces. The main Iraqi positions were around Fallujah by this stage. The Habbaniya's garrison, supported by units from *Kingcol*, advanced on the Iraqi positions at Fallujah at 1445 hours on 19 May. They encountered very little opposition and took 300 prisoners. British forces were also warned on this day that they were to prepare to move into Syria at short notice. Later on in the day attacks were made against Mezze airfield, near Damascus. A Ju52 was destroyed and an He111 and a Ju90 that had been damaged on 15 May received more hits. A number of French aircraft were also hit in this attack. As a result, three German airmen and a French soldier were wounded.

What remained of the German Air Force was thrown at Fallujah on 20 May. The first encounter took place when an Bf110 was driven off by three Gladiators. A little later a pair of Hurricanes broke up the attack of four more Bf110s. The Germans could claim a victory that day when *Leutnant* Martin Drewes shot down an Audax flown by Sergeant Smith. There were more aerial combats during the day, with a procession of German aircraft strafing British forward positions in the Fallujah area. It was a shoestring air war because by the close of 20 May the nine British fighters that were available had flown twenty-six sorties between them. Five Hurricanes belonging to 208 and 112 Squadrons had taken the opportunity to attack Mezze airfield in the early morning of 20 May. They had shot up six French aircraft and fifty vehicles.

The British were cycling units through this theatre in order to keep up their commitments elsewhere. The RAF bomber strength in Palestine was growing. They could now attack French airfields in Syria at will.

By 22 May there were thirteen Gladiators, five Hurricanes, fourteen Blenheims and a number of serviceable Oxfords, Audaxes and Gordons at Habbaniya. There were Lysanders in Transjordan; Blenheims, Bombays and Valentias in Palestine; and Vincents, Valentias, Douglas DC2s and Aw Atalantas in Southern Iraq. There were also Swordfish available from HMS *Hermes*.

Despite the fact that the German aircraft had taken quite a beating, there was other help on its way for the Iraqis. The French had always been averse to allowing Italian aircraft to use Syria as a staging post. But by 23 May an agreement had finally been hammered out. *Capitano* Francesco Sforza, at the head of twelve Fiat CR42 biplanes, left Italy bound for Greece. The formation refuelled and flew on to Rhodes, although one of the CR42s crashed during the flight. The remaining eleven CR42s arrived at Aleppo on Sunday 25 May 1941. They remained there overnight, flying on to Mosul and then to Kirkuk, where they would make strafing attacks on British forces, moving from Fallujah towards Baghdad.

Meanwhile, on 24 May, a Valentia of 216 Squadron, flown by Flight Lieutenant Bartlett, landed thirteen sappers in Syria, to the west of Campaniya. The sappers spent three quarters of an hour laying charges and then destroying an important bridge on the Aleppo to Mosul railway line. As Bartlett was taking off, a French armoured car arrived and opened up. Bartlett managed to escape unharmed and for his actions he was later awarded the Distinguished Flying Cross. On the same afternoon a Blenheim belonging to 211 Squadron, on a reconnaissance over Syria, was chased by a pair of Morane 406s.

The Vichy French authorities in Syria were becoming increasingly alarmed at the fact that the RAF could fly in and attack with impunity. They requested reinforcements but these would take a day or two to arrive.

On 28 May a second major train load of supplies arrived via Syria, at Mosul. This time there was heavier artillery in the shape of eight 155 mm guns, with 6,000 rounds, over 350 machine pistols, 30,000 grenades and 32 trucks.

On the same day a Blenheim of 211 Squadron, on a reconnaissance flight over Aleppo, was attacked by French fighters. The Blenheim, flown by Sergeant David, had left Aqir, where there was an RAF airbase. Aqir is some 9 km to the south-west of Ramla in Palestine. The Blenheim was shot down by *Sous Lieutenant* Vuillemin and David and his crew were all killed.

The French Moranes were also in action during the evening, out of Nerab in eastern Syria. They were escorting four Ju52s. During the course of the day twenty-four Dewoitine D520 fighters, belonging to GCIII/6, flew in to Syria from Algeria. They had left their base in Algeria four days before and had flown around the north coast of the Mediterranean. Two of the aircraft had force-landed in Turkey; one of them crashed, killing the pilot and the Turks interned the other pilot.

On the ground the situation was becoming critical for the Iraqis and the British were moving up more troops, such as a battalion of Ghurkha rifles, flown in from Basra to Habbaniya on 29 May. *Habforce* was just outside of Baghdad by 30 May. At this point Rashid Ali threw in the towel and fled. It fell to the mayor of Baghdad to request a truce and negotiate surrender terms.

On the following day, however, a Blenheim of 211 Squadron flew a sortie into Syria. Lieutenant de la Taille and *Sergeant Chef* Veillie of GCI/7 intercepted the Blenheim flown by Pilot Officer Hooper near Aleppo. Hooper managed to escape, but had to jettison his bombs in the process.

The Italians began to pack up to leave and were ready to go. The ground staff clambered on board an S79 and the rest of the men got into two buses. The CR42s covered the retreat to Aleppo, where a German officer met them. It was to be a few days before the unit could return to Rhodes, but they achieved this on 5 June, after a flight of three hours and forty minutes. The aircraft were once again over-painted, back to Italian markings.

The Germans, meanwhile, were far less fortunate. They had suffered significantly and had lost all fourteen of the original Bf110s, five He111s and a large number of the transport aircraft that had remained. In fact, according to German sources, Grobba contacted Berlin in panic on 28 May 1941, by which stage Baghdad had not yet fallen to the British. He reported that none of the Bf110s were serviceable and he only had a pair of He111s with four bombs between them. What remained of the German effort to support the 'Arab Freedom Movement in the Middle East' (as described in Führer Directive No. 30, 23 May 1941) left Iraq during the night of 29 May 1941. Grobba fled Iraq on the following day.

Abandoned by its erstwhile allies, the Vichy *Armée du Levant* was left alone. They could easily see what was going to happen and that it would only be a matter of time before British and Commonwealth forces advanced. General de Verdilhac, the Vichy commander in chief, reported on 28 May: 'Concentration of Australian and English troops in Palestine frontier area northwest of Safad. Strength 6,000 to 7,000 men with artillery, trucks, armoured cars. No tracked vehicles.'

De Verdilhac could not have been more incorrect. In fact, Operation *Exporter*, commanded by Jumbo Wilson, based in Jerusalem, would involve 35,000 men.

Chapter Four

Operation *Exporter* – Phase One

In the aftermath of the Ottoman Turk defeat in 1918 both Syria and Lebanon, former parts of the Turkish Empire, had been placed under French mandate. It should have come as no great surprise to the French that the mere fact that Syria had been used as a jumping off point for both German and Italian aircraft in Iraq, and they had allowed it to be used to resupply Iraqi ground forces, meant that it would come under immediate attack by British and Commonwealth troops. In fact, the French in Syria, following the armistice in June 1940, had been happy to fall in line with the Vichy government.

Back in October 1940 General Georges Catroux had been sent by de Gaulle to Egypt. He was charged with fighting the Free French corner, which claimed that Syria could easily fall and become Free French. At the time there was a pro-Vichy high commissioner in Syria, General Henri Dentz, which meant that much of what Catroux had claimed about Syria would be negated by Dentz's tough stance.

There was also a concern, as far as the British could see, that having jumped to the aid of Greece in their war against the Italians, the Germans had been only too prepared to support their allies, which had ultimately led to defeat both on the Greek mainland and the loss of Crete. It should also be borne in mind that there were still considerable German paratrooper concentrations in the central eastern Mediterranean. There was a distinct possibility that if British and Commonwealth troops invaded Syria then, at the very least, the Germans would send paratroopers to assist Dentz. Comparatively speaking, Britain was weak in the eastern Mediterranean.

The Turks were also jittery. They, too, believed that there was a serious possibility of Germans arriving in force in Syria. The Turks had moved troops up to their frontier with Syria.

Nonetheless, Winston Churchill overruled all of the objections. He knew that he was spreading his men thinly, needing them in North Africa to protect Egypt and the Suez Canal. It was not going to be an easy operation. Comparatively speaking, the Vichy forces in Syria were strong, in addition to which there was a small naval force. The French had also strengthened their air force in the region.

According to Gavin Long in *Australia in the War of 1939–1945 Series 1 – Army – Volume II – Greece, Crete and Syria* (1st edition, 1953):

> The Vichy French army was believed to include six regiments of regulars, including one of the Foreign Legion, one of mixed colonial and metropolitan troops, and four of African natives. There were also about 9,000 cavalry, some units being horsed and others equipped with tanks or armoured cars, ninety field and medium guns, and some 10,000 Levantine infantry of doubtful value. Thus, leaving out of account the Levantine troops, there was the equivalent of two strong infantry divisions and a half-division of tanks, armoured cars and cavalry – 35,000 regulars in all, including some 8,000 Frenchmen. Under Dentz, General de Verdilhac was deputy commander-in-chief; the three principal area commanders were General Delhomme at Damascus, Colonel Beucler at Beirut, and Colonel Rottier at Aleppo. General Jennequin commanded the air force.
>
> The main components of the invading force were to be the 7th Australian Division, hitherto untried in battle but strenuously trained since its formation in April and May 1940; the veteran 5th Indian Brigade, recently withdrawn from Abyssinia; and the Free French contingent, which was in process of being organized into six battalions, two batteries of 75s, one tank company, and Colonel Collet's cavalry detachment. The air force made available by Air Marshal Tedder to support the invasion consisted of two fighter squadrons and a half (including No. 3 R.A.A.F.), two bomber squadrons and one army cooperation squadron. These were commanded by Air

Commodore L.O. Brown and possessed some seventy first-line aircraft; the French had nearly 100, including sixty fighters. While the military operation was being planned part of the British air force had continued almost daily to bomb Syrian airfields. To support the advance on the coastal plain and protect it against interference by the French naval force, which included two 3,000-ton destroyers and three submarines, Admiral Cunningham allotted, at the outset, two cruisers and four destroyers under Vice-Admiral King of the 15th Cruiser Squadron. A second naval force – the landing ship *Glengyle*, cruiser *Coventry*, and two destroyers – was to be available to land troops on the Syrian coast. Thus all the serviceable cruisers and six out of about seventeen serviceable destroyers were allotted to the Syrian operation.

Wilson's primary objectives were to take the airfields at Damascus, Beirut and Rayak. Wavell believed that the force that had been allocated to Wilson was woefully inadequate. He was of the opinion that all that could be achieved was to take some border airfield objectives and then launch raids towards Tripoli and Homs. He felt that the French would dig in around Aleppo and Mosul and then launch a counterattack.

The Turks had been approached to assist in occupying Syria. It should be pointed out that Lebanon at this stage, although technically remaining a separate entity, was, in fact, administered by the French, together with Syria. The Turks turned down the suggestion on 2 June 1941 and the Imperial Defence Committee in London made the decision that Syria was now the principal objective. This was despite the fact that some believed that the Germans were about to make an attack in the same way as they had dealt with Crete, on Cyprus.

Wilson's force was to attack on three fronts; the principal objective of all three columns was Beirut. One column would aim for Deraa and then move on to Damascus. This would be spearheaded by the 5th Indian Brigade, under Brigadier W.L. Lloyd. These forces would then halt at Deraa and the Free French would take over, pushing on towards Damascus. Meanwhile, a smaller force would hit Merjayoun and then Rayak. The main force, spearheaded by

Major General J.D. Lavarack's 7th Australian Division and supported by the Special Service Brigade and elements of the Cavalry Division and the 6th Division, would advance up the coast towards Beirut.

In addition to the Vichy ground forces and a small naval force operating out of Beirut and Tripoli, the French Air Force had been greatly strengthened. A number of Potez 25s were already in Syria and Lebanon. But *Groupe de Chasse* I/7 had arrived between 31 January and 5 March 1940 with twenty-six Morane 406s. By September 1940, twelve Martin 167F bombers belonging to *Groupe de Bombardement* I/39 were also in Syria. A training unit linked to this force, *Escadrille* 3/39, had been established, with six Bloch MB200 bombers. A number of Potez 63-11 aircraft had been sent for reconnaissance work, which now meant that the French had five *Escadrilles* observation units, four with six Potez 25TOEs and one with four. There was also a French naval air force unit, which had Loire 130 flying boats. The newest arrivals, as we have already seen, were the Dewoitine D520s, of which twenty-five were established at Rayak. This meant that the Vichy French Air Force, supported by the navy, was a fairly potent force by 7 June 1941.

The French had been alert to both the ground and air threat. On 2 June a Blenheim belonging to 11 Squadron had been chased over the Palmyra, Aleppo, area and then out to sea by Morane 406s. The pilot had had to use his outer fuel tanks and found that the fuel cocks had jammed. As a result he had to force land on a beach at Rouviani.

Precisely why can only be speculated, but Dentz demanded that both German and Italian aircraft leave Syria no later than 5 June. As we already know, the Italians left for Rhodes on that very day. We can only speculate that Dentz did not want to provoke the RAF into additional air attacks on his precious airfields. This empty-handed gesture was to prove to be worthless, as on 5 June three Blenheims from 11 Squadron spotted CR42s and S79s on the ground at Aleppo airfield. *Adjutant Chef* Georges Amerger of GCI/7 led three Morane 406s to see off the Blenheims. But they were unable to intercept them.

In fact, this was to be very much the blueprint for many of the engagements between the RAF and the Vichy French over Syria

...chy Morane D406s which were used as advanced trainers. These still have their original squadron ...arkings.

...520 of GCI/3 with the fuselage bar painted as an arrow. Note the red viper on the white pennant. ...e unit, as GCIII/3 was in action over Oran on 8 November 1942.

...rre Le Gloan in his D 520 of GC III/6.

A D520 in France. The nose is yellow and the tail has red and white stripes.

Three D 520s of GC III/6 on an airfield at Algiers before they were shipped out to Syria.

A Morane 406 probably belonging to GC I/7 in Syria.

Martin M167F of Aeronavale
[Flo]tille 4F on a Greek airfield
[en] route from North Africa to Syria.

A pilot from GC II/8 standing in
front of his Bloch MB152.

A LeO 451 from GB I/31 in Syria. This aircraft was destroyed on the ground on 2 July 1941.

A Potez 63-11 and two Morane 406s about to be set alight by a group of RAF, Australians and two French officers at the conclusion of the Syrian campaign.

burning Potez 63-11 with
Morane 406 on fire in the
background. Presumably,
the photograph was taken
the end of hostilities in
Syria.

Australian troops
cautiously advance beside
a rock face in Syria ever
watchful of Vichy air
attack.

Australian infantry advancing in open order across Syrian terrain.

Burnt out Vichy armoured cars in Syria.

That was left of the tank and motor workshops at the Renault works at Billancourt after the RAF bombed the factory on 3 March 1942. Note the lorries parked on the roadside on each side of the factory.

Vichy French inspect a shot down Swordfish from HMS *Ark Royal* in Dakar in September 1940.

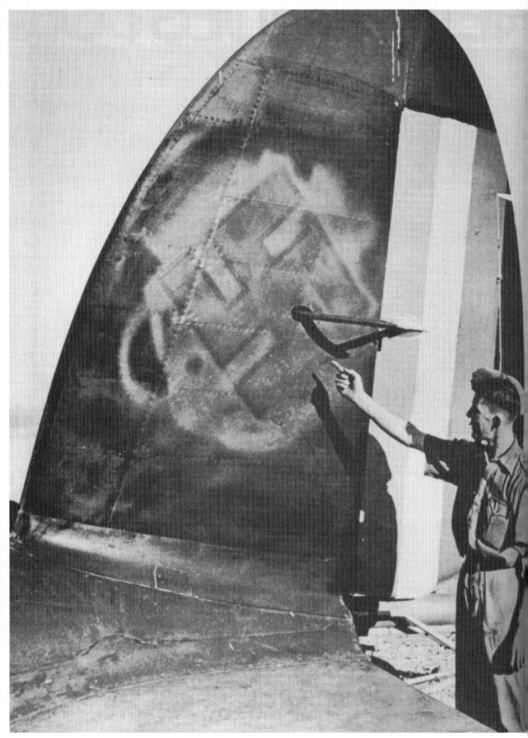

The tell-tale signs of German involvement in Syria. A poorly overpainted swastika and Vichy colours added to the rudder on this downed aircraft.

AAF Fairey Battles in formation.

Valentia biplane used during the air campaigns against the Vichy.

An SAAF Gloster Gladiator.

An Italian CR 42.

General Dentz, Vichy commander in Syria.

General Wilson signs the armistice agreement in Syria watched by General Catroux and the Vichy delegates.

A Junkers 90 with repainted Iraqi markings on the way to the Middle East using Vichy Syria as a staging post. Note the Ju52 in the background.

A clearer shot of the Ju90 with the Iraqi markings.

A shot down He 111 with disguised Luftwaffe markings and over painted Iraqi or Vichy French markings.

The LeO 451 flown by Commandant Lauzin of GB i/31 in Syria. The aircraft was destroyed on 11 June 1941.

Capitaine Jacobi of GCIII/6 with his Dewoitine 520 at Brindisi in May 1941. Jacobi was later shot down and killed by anti-aircraft fire on 12 June.

A close up of the markings on a Martin M167F of Aeronavale Escadrille 6B in Syria.

LeO 451s of GB I/25, the closest to the camera is No. 197 that was destroyed in an accident on
June, 1941.

Potez 650 transports belonging to GT II/15.

An Amiot 143 of Groupement de la 38 Escadre used in the attempted airlift of troops from mainland France to Syria in June 1941.

during the campaign. The French were incredibly tardy in taking off and would usually only respond as the first bombs began dropping on their airfields.

On 6 June 1941 a Vichy Martin 167F dropped leaflets in French on Haifa airfield. It is believed that the pilot of this aircraft was formerly Free French but he had defected to Vichy. The Vichy French also sent another Martin, flown by Commandant Ader, who was the commanding officer of GBI/39, on a reconnaissance flight over Cyprus.

On the last day before Operation *Exporter* was launched a number of Morane 406s, led by *Adjutant Chef* Veillie, intercepted Flying Officer Holdsworth's long-range Hurricane of A Flight, 208 Squadron. They managed to do some superficial damage.

The US Council in Beirut received a message from Lieutenant Colonel Montrelay, of the Vichy authorities in Syria, stating that there were no more Germans or Italians in the territory on 7 June. Montrelay maintained that if the RAF launched any more attacks on Syria or Lebanon then these would be considered an act of war. But it was far too late for any blustering threats from the isolated Vichy territory. Operation *Exporter* was launched at 0230 hours on 8 June 1941.

As a side note in history, one of the Jewish guides that had crossed into Vichy territory five hours before zero hour was Moshe Dayan. Dayan was a member of the full-time, professional arm of the Zionist underground militia. They had been effectively at war with the British in Palestine. But now they had negotiated a truce for the duration of the Second World War. Dayan was keen to show how valuable his men could be to the British, in the hope that this would stand them in good stead for negotiations once hostilities had ended.

Dayan's Jewish and Arab guides were tasked with securing bridges and disarming demolition charges. After they had achieved this they had made for a stone-built two-storey French police building about a mile away. They stormed the building after Dayan had thrown a grenade through an open window. The men then carried a heavy machine gun and a mortar up onto the roof. All they could do was to wait until the Australian troops, under Brigadier Jack Edwin Stawell Stevens, pushed through to link up with them.

In the meantime, fresh French troops began to surround the police station. Dayan manned the machine gun on the roof. As soon as he began firing the French returned fire. Dayan took out his field glasses to try and spot the location of the enemy fire. He was trying to focus them when a bullet hit the binoculars, splintered the lens and the metal casing, which embedded itself into the socket of Dayan's left eye. Momentarily Dayan passed out but when he regained consciousness he found he was on a stretcher and he had also suffered a hand wound. With no painkilling drugs he was in enormous amounts of pain. An Australian officer, worried that Dayan would die due to blood loss, suggested he be turned over to the French. But Dayan was adamant that he would remain in the police station and that they could hold off the French until reinforcements arrived.

By the time Stevens' men reached them the besieged had actually captured several French trucks and a number of prisoners. Some twelve hours after he had been wounded, Dayan was told at Haifa hospital that he would survive, but he would lose his left eye.

According to John Herington's *Australia in the War of 1939–1945 Series 3 – Air - Volume III – Air War Against Germany and Italy, 1939– 1943* (1st edition, 1954):

A British offensive in the Western Desert designed to relieve Tobruk was already projected for mid-June, so both land and air forces available for a Syrian expedition were small. One light-bomber, one army-cooperation, one Fleet Air Arm, and two and a half fighter squadrons were initially under the command of Air Commodore Brown, air officer commanding in Palestine and Transjordan, though he could call, if necessary, on No. 84 (Blenheim) Squadron in Iraq and the heavy bombers based in Egypt. The total number of aircraft immediately available was seventy and there was some doubt whether No. 3 Squadron R.A.A.F., which had suffered a plethora of accidents and setbacks during its conversion to Tomahawks, would be ready, but fortunately these difficulties were overcome in time. Action by these small forces against a French air force and army, numerically superior, far stronger in tanks and capable of reinforcement from France or the Balkans, contained all the elements of a gamble, but it was hoped that divided loyalties and lack of purpose would detract from French resistance.

For No. 3 Squadron the Syrian campaign opened with an attack by five Tomahawks on Rayak satellite airfield at 6.15am on 8th June. The pilots found no French aircraft in the air, but shot up six Morane fighters on the ground. The same evening four Tomahawks escorted Blenheims attacking oil tanks at Beirut. Until the 21st the squadron was constantly switched from one pressing duty to another, according to priorities determined by Air Headquarters Palestine and Transjordan. During this period 199 sorties, an average of fifteen daily, were flown with varying emphasis on interception duties; naval patrols; tactical reconnaissance; strafing of enemy land forces; protective patrols over forward troops; bomber-escort duties and escort for reconnoitring Gladiators.'

In fact, the first air combat in the campaign involved three Hurricanes belonging to 80 Squadron. They made for Rayak in order to shoot up GBI/39's Martin 167Fs. By the time they got there the unit had already moved to Madjaloun. Instead, they bombed French columns near Kuneitra.

The Tomahawks of No. 3 Squadron RAAF were, in fact, on their first operational sortie. The French mistook them for Dewoitine 520s and, consequently, when the Tomahawks made their attack it was a complete surprise to the French ground spotters. Herington could be mistaken in believing that they were Moranes, as GCIII/6 was supplied with Dewoitine 520s. *Sous Lieutenant* Pierre Le Gloan of GCII/6 was aloft with six Dewoitine 520s, heading for Damascus.

By midday Le Gloan and *Sergeant Chef* Mertzisen were once again aloft, escorting a Potez 63-11 belonging to GRII/39. They were tasked with making a reconnaissance around Ezraa. The three aircraft spotted a British motorized column. The two Dewoitine 520s came in to strafe the vehicles. Mertzisen's machine was hit and he crash-landed, but managed to escape on foot, returning to his unit with the help of some locals. Le Gloan gained height again to protect the Potez as it began its flight home.

Meanwhile, a Hurricane belonging to A Flight of 208 Squadron, piloted by Flight Lieutenant J.R. Aldis, was flying a long-range reconnaissance over the Damascus area. Le Gloan peeled off from his escort and shot down the Hurricane. This was his twelfth victim of the war.

Le Gloan is a very interesting character. He had joined the French Air Force at the age of eighteen and had shot down his first enemy aircraft, a Dornier 17, on 23 November 1939. During the battle of France he claimed another three German bombers. By June 1940 he was operating out of Le Luc airfield, piloting a Dewoitine 520. On 13 June, after the Italians had declared war, he shot down a pair of Fiat BR20 bombers. Two days later, accompanied by one other pilot, Le Gloan took on twelve Fiat CR42s and shot down three of them. On his return flight to his airfield he claimed another CR42 and a BR20 bomber. He was immediately promoted to second lieutenant. His squadron, GCIII/6, was withdrawn to Algiers on 20 June 1940. In May 1941 the unit was transferred to Syria and by the end of the Syrian campaign Le Gloan would have claimed six Hurricanes and one Gloster Gladiator. By 1943 Le Gloan was no longer fighting for the Vichy, but instead for the Free French. The unit was renamed GC3/6 Roussillon and was now flying P39 Airacobra fighters. On 11 September 1943 Le Gloan's aircraft developed engine problems. He tried to make a forced landing on the shoreline, but as his aircraft hit the ground the underbelly fuel tank exploded. Le Gloan was killed instantly. He must be one of the few pilots of the war that is credited with shooting down both German and Italian aircraft, as well as British ones.

In terms of aerial activity 8 June 1941 was an incredibly busy day. Le Gloan was on another escort sortie between Damascus and Mezze in the afternoon. An accompanying Dewoitine 520, flown by *Sergeant Chef* Ravily, crashed on the edge of the airfield after only having gained 200 m in altitude. The pilot was killed.

Another pair of Dewoitine 520s, at around 1300 hours, encountered some Fulmars belonging to 803 Squadron. They were protecting Royal Navy cruisers off Sidon. The two French pilots, Lieutenant Martin and *Sous Lieutenant* Brondel, both of GCIII/6, believed that the aircraft were, in fact, Hurricanes. Martin attacked first, but he was shot down and had to bale out over the coast, where Australian troops captured him. Brondel, seeing what had become of his colleague, returned to base and reported that a fighter had shot down Martin. In actual fact, anti-aircraft gunners from the cruiser squadron had made the kill.

Six more Dewoitine 520s of GCIII/6 mistook Fulmars as Hurricanes. It was at around 1532 hours. The six French pilots *Capitaine* Leon Richard, *Sous Lieutenant* Rivory, Sergeant Michaux, Lieutenant Stenou, Lieutenant Boiries and *Sous Lieutenant* Satgé, engaged half a dozen Fulmars. The French claimed two kills in the engagement, but several of the French fighters were damaged as a result of the air combat and anti-aircraft fire from the Royal Navy vessels below.

In fact, 803 Squadron had suffered very badly during the course of the day. Lieutenant J.M. Christian and his observer, Sub-lieutenant N. Cullen, had both been killed, so too had Petty Officer J.A. Gardner and Leading Airman H. Pickering. Certainly, a third Fulmar had been shot down, but the two crewmembers had been picked up. Two more Fulmars had been badly damaged. It was clear that if the French were going to launch more attacks against the Royal Navy then better air protection would be needed.

One of the pilots belonging to 80 Squadron and flying a Hurricane assigned for this duty was none other than Pilot Officer Roald Dahl. He had originally been flying Gloster Gladiators and had made a forced landing in an attempt to find a desert airstrip on 19 September 1940. He had been very badly injured and, in fact, had fractured his skull and was temporarily blinded. Once he had recovered he was passed fit for flying duty in February 1941. He rejoined his unit in time to be involved in the Greek campaign, being based at Eleusina, to the north-west of the centre of Athens. Dahl's first aerial combat took place on 15 April, when he attacked half a dozen Ju88s that were bombing shipping. He shot one down and in another engagement a day later he claimed a second Ju88. As Greece was overrun Dahl was one of a handful of British pilots to get their aircraft off the mainland. He flew to Crete and a month later to Egypt. The squadron reassembled at Haifa. The following incident on 8 June 1941 is disputed by the French and Dahl was credited with a probable kill. He apparently intercepted a Potez 63 at around 1630 hours and shot up the Vichy aircraft, setting one of its engines on fire. Dahl believed that the aircraft then dived into the sea. The French have never confirmed whether or not this was the case. For Dahl this was his penultimate kill, as on 15 June he was able to claim a Ju88.

Shortly after this, as a result of the injuries he had suffered the previous September, he began to get severe headaches that caused him to blackout. He was subsequently invalided home.

Elsewhere on 8 June 1941 six Vichy Martin 167Fs made attacks along the coast at Sheikh Meskine. By the end of day two of the campaign it was readily apparent that not only were the Vichy troops prepared to fight, but that they were more than a match for the limited resources that the British had thrown into the campaign. In fact, the three-pronged offensive had pretty much failed to make any impression.

The Australians and 11 Commando had managed to cross the Litani River in the south. In the centre, the Australian Brigade had advanced around ten miles and had only reached Merjayoun. In the Golan Heights area the Shehab Bridge had been captured by units of the 5th Indian Brigade. This would leave the road towards Damascus open, but it would mean capturing Deraa and then pushing on to the capital some sixty miles away.

By the night of 9 June 1941, advanced elements of the 1st Royal Fusiliers were pushing towards Damascus, which was now forty miles away. The French troops in Deraa put up quite a fight until a battery of 25-pdrs was brought up and the French garrison escaped by train. Once Deraa had been taken Indian units moved to take the hilltop village of Sheikh Meskin. Here, the French were well dug in with machine guns and artillery. The first attack was repulsed with heavy losses, but the French were eventually ousted from the area. In fact, the Vichy defenders were evacuated under cover of air attacks. It was now the job of the Free French Brigade to take up the advance. By the end of the day the French had managed to get to within around ten miles of Damascus, but Vichy French resistance was stiffening.

The bulk of the air combat took place on 9 June around the coastal area. Attacks were made by French bombers on the 15th Cruiser Squadron. Meanwhile, two Vichy destroyers shelled Australian positions in the Litani area. In the ensuing fight a pair of British destroyers, HMS *Jackal* and HMS *Janus*, were both badly damaged. Flying Officer G.H. Westlake of 80 Squadron also claimed a Potez 63, as Dahl had done the day before, but, once again, this loss has been always disputed by the French.

At around 1420 hours on 9 June three of 80 Squadron's Hurricanes were on patrol over the cruiser squadron when they spotted a large number of Vichy aircraft approaching. Half a dozen Dewoitine 520s from GCIII/6 were escorting four Bloch MB200s belonging to EB3/39 and six Martin 167Fs of GBI/39. The French aircraft came in to attack the cruiser squadron at around 1525 hours. Flight Lieutenant J. Lockhart, who was leading the section of three Hurricanes, led an attack against the MB200s, but had not noticed the Dewoitines, which were flying at a higher altitude. Lockhart came in out of the sun and shot up the leading bomber. It turned towards Beirut, obviously badly damaged. It then went into a dive and it was reported that it crashed into the sea. There was also a report that a parachute had been seen.

Sous Lieutenant Le Gloan led two other Dewoitine 520s in an attack on the Hurricanes. He shot down one of them and saw the pilot bale out. Sergeant Mequet engaged one of the other Hurricanes. Le Gloan then saw Mequet behind a second Hurricane, but Mequet had to break off as he was out of ammunition. Le Gloan took over and shot the Hurricane down, once again seeing the pilot bale out. Le Gloan had managed to shoot down both of Lockhart's colleagues. He had, in fact, killed Pilot Officer Lynch and Pilot Officer Crowther. It later transpired that two of the Bloch MB200s had been lost in the attack. Adjutant de Riverleux de Varax, Adjutant Idier and Sergeant Orgueil had died when one of the Blochs had crashed into the sea. The parachute that had been seen by Lockhart had conveyed Sergeant Seize to safety. He was the only crewman to survive from that aircraft. The second Bloch, which had been badly shot up, crash-landed close to Bir Hassen and none of the crew was injured.

There was further air combat in the same area on the same day and the events partially dovetail into the combat that had just taken place. At exactly the same time, at 1540 hours, *Capitaine* Richard had led three Dewoitine 520s out of Rayak, following a report by Le Gloan. At the same time three Hurricanes had taken off to take up Lockhart's position and relieve them. As the six aircraft approached the area it was the Hurricane pilots that got the drop and attacked. Flying Officer Westlake zeroed in on one of the Dewoitines and claimed that he shot it down. He then assisted Sergeant R.T. Wallace to shoot up a second one. They saw the Dewoitine's propeller stop, then the aircraft burst into flames and fell into the sea. *Capitaine* Richard, meanwhile, chased a Hurricane almost down to sea level, where it disappeared. He then came under fire, which caused a burst of flame as the electrical circuits were shot up. This may well have been the second aircraft that Westlake and Wallace had attacked. Richard managed to gain control of his aircraft and joined Sergeant Michaux, who was also later to claim a Hurricane in the dogfight. There was a head-on collision between a Dewoitine flown by *Sous Lieutenant* Rivory and Sergeant M.W. Bennett's Hurricane. Bennett, although badly burned, was picked up by the Royal Navy and Rivory was taken prisoner.

The French also launched ground attacks on Allied troops on the road to Damascus. Three Potez 25TOEs belonging to EO594 were escorted by two Morane 406s of GCI/7. Both of the Moranes were hit by ground fire.

9 June also saw the first sortie launched by *Aeronavale Escadrille* 19S. The sortie was launched by the commanding officer of the unit, Lieutenant de V. Brossier. He was flying a Loire 130 19S-6 on a reconnaissance mission over Famagusta on Cyprus. At around 1800 hours he dropped a pair of bombs on a merchant ship just off Cape Greco. The ship fired back, putting some holes in the aircraft.

There was considerable pressure on the limited air assets of the British by 10 June. It was therefore decided that the Fulmars of 803 Squadron would have to take responsibility for protecting the fleet, as the Hurricanes were needed to protect the ground forces.

On the ground Merjayoun was taken by the 25th Australian Infantry Brigade and the 21st Australian Infantry Brigade had pushed across the Litani River and linked up with British commandos. They would push on and reach Sidon in two days.

The French were flying in reinforcements. Nine Loire et Olivier LeO451 bombers belonging to GBI/31 made it to Aleppo. Along with them were four Farman transports belonging to GTI/15 with the ground crews on board. The whole unit, commanded by Commandant Lauzin, had flown from Istres to Brindisi and then on to Aleppo. Four of the bombers had dropped out during the journey; all but one of them would finally make it to Syria. The French were also planning other reinforcements. The training school at Aulnot was sending four Morane 406s and ten Dewoitine 520s were authorized to be sent to be Syria. These were from GCI/2.

The British were also planning reinforcements. Half a dozen Albacores belonging to 829 Squadron from HMS *Formidable* arrived at Lydda. Another unit, which was to become 127 Squadron, commanded by Flight Lieutenant J.M. Bodman, was forming up at Habbaniya. They were initially supplied with four Mark I Hurricanes and a pair of long-range Hurricanes. The Mark I Hurricanes were all second-hand. Two had been part of the defence of Malta and had belonged to 94 Squadron. The British also managed to scrape up four Gladiators.

Meanwhile, over the Damascus and Deraa area, Martin 167Fs belonging to GBI/39 were intercepted by a pair of 3 RAAF Squadron's Tomahawks. In fact, the M167F that they found was actually over Palestinian air space. The aircraft was being flown by *Sous Lieutenant* Causson. The Tomahawks did not claim him as he was shot down by anti-aircraft fire. The French also threw aircraft at Allied columns on the Damascus road and against the Royal Navy fleet off Sidon. The French made the decision also to abandon Mezze airfield, near Damascus. This meant that GRII/39 withdrew to Baalbeck-la Colonne.

The French naval aircraft launched attacks on merchant ships and during the night of 10 June three Bloch MB200s belonging to EB3/39, escorted by nine Potez 25TOEs (EO593 and EO594), bombed British troop concentrations to the south of Sanamein.

The British were in a considerable quandary; the Royal Navy had to be protected and they were not only being attacked by the French, but also by German Ju88s operating out of Rhodes. Unbeknown to the British, de Verdilhac was planning a major counter offensive, aiming to hit the British at their three weakest points. It would be a few days before this counterattack developed, but in the meantime it was the British that had momentum with them to a degree.

The Free French ground forces were now in the Kissoué area and they came under strafing attacks from Morane 406s of GCI/7. Later in the day this French unit was ordered to pull back from Estabel and re-establish itself at Homs. However, the Vichy French would discover that this airfield was too far away from the front and consequently ordered *Capitaine* Polikow to take six aircraft on detachment, to be based at Rayak.

Eleven sorties were launched by M167Fs of GBI/39 on 11 June, which included attacks on British columns on the Damascus road. During one of these attacks an aircraft flown by Lieutenant Duparchy was hit by anti-aircraft fire. He managed to nurse his aircraft on just one engine back to Palmyra. Four Loiré et Olivier LeO451s of GBI/31 took off at 1920 hours. They were due to rendezvous with Dewoitine 520s as their escort, but the fighters arrived too late. The LeO451s pressed home their attack, bombing Allied vehicles to the south of Damascus. By the time they had completed their mission it was dark. The commanding officer, Commandant Lauzin, made the decision to land at Mezze. He had no idea that the airfield had been abandoned by the Vichy French and that they had left obstacles on the landing strips before retreating. Three of the bombers, as they came in to land, were destroyed.

Pilot Officer Bill Vale of 80 Squadron claimed a Potez 63 whilst flying his Hurricane on a sortie during the day. This is another engagement that is hotly disputed. A Potez 63 of GRII/39, flown by *Capitaine* Forget, was shot up but not shot down on a reconnaissance mission on 11 June. Vale's probable victim was another reported crash, involving a Dewoitine 520, which had come down near Haifa. Once again, the French records suggest that no aircraft were lost on 11 June.

Another busy day in the skies over Syria was 12 June 1941. At 0600 hours Flying Officer Holdsworth and Flying Officer Macrostie of A Flight, 208 Squadron, flying Hurricanes, were sent out on a strafing attack on the road to the north of Merjayoun. The two aircraft had flown to the landing ground at Roshpina. As the two Hurricanes came in to make their strafing attacks, Macrostie's Hurricane was hit by ground fire and he crash-landed. A Lysander picked him up the next day. Holdsworth's aircraft had also been damaged in the attack.

The French were also out on strafing attacks, targeting the area around Sanamein. It was about the same time of the day. GCIII/6 had sent three Dewoitine 520s to escort a single Potez 63 belonging to GAO583. Morane 406s of GCI/7 strafed a British camp near

Deraa, along with a Potez 63 of GRII/39. There were further attacks by GBI/39. Five of their Martin M167Fs were hit by anti-aircraft fire as they bombed British vehicles to the north-east of Merjayoun.

The first engagement of the afternoon fell to the British. No. 11 Squadron had launched six Blenheims to attack French positions to the south of Kissoué. At roughly the same time Pilot Officer Vale's Hurricane developed severe engine problems. He wrote off his aircraft when he crash-landed at Tyr.

As already noted, the Germans were also committed to engaging the Royal Navy off the coast. Eight Tomahawks belonging to 3 RAAF Squadron, aloft at around 1450 hours, identified what they believed to be eight Italian aircraft. They were, in fact, Ju88s; there were eight of them and they were trying to attack the Royal Navy vessels. Squadron Leader Peter Jeffrey, Flight Lieutenant J.R. Perrin and Flying Officer J.W.H. Saunders all claimed a kill. These Ju88s were not from Rhodes and neither were they Italian. They had been flown in from Crete. In fact, the German records would later confirm that two of their Ju88s failed to return to base. These were the ones flown by *Leutnant* H. Dickjobst and *Leutnant* R. Bennewitz.

Shortly after this, at around 1609, Commandant Jacobi led a flight of Dewoitine 520s of GCIII/6 on a reconnaissance mission around the Deraa and Hasbaya area. They came under fire and three of the fighters were hit by ground forces. Jacobi crash-landed to the south of Sidon and was killed in the incident. *Sergeant Chef* Moribot's aircraft was also badly damaged and crashed on landing at Rayak, but he was not injured. Sergeant Coisneau was hit in the face by ground fire, but he managed to coax his aircraft home.

Blenheims were sent out to bomb Rayak airfield at 1800 hours. They were escorted by half a dozen Hurricanes of 80 Squadron. As the aircraft came in to attack, a pair of the Hurricanes split off to engage two Potez 63s of GAO583. *Sous Lieutenant* Tatraux's aircraft was hit in the starboard engine by Sergeant R.T. Wallace. Tatraux's aircraft fired back and hit Wallace's Hurricane, causing him to break off the attack. Both Tatraux's aircraft and the one flown by *Capitaine* d'Argoubet managed to get back to base.

Despite the disastrous first missions on 11 June, four LeO451s of GBI/31 were out attacking British positions near Sanamein at dusk. Once again, they had problems as they came into land at Rayak, when the aircraft flown by *Sous Lieutenant* Bornesque crashed as he attempted to land.

The French were particularly concerned about the progress of the Australian troops on the coast and the fact that so far very little damage had been caused to the Royal Navy vessels. General Dentz requested via Admiral Darlan that the Germans launch a Ju87 Stuka attack on the Royal Navy vessels. Darlan was confident that the Vichy French had the assets to carry out the job themselves and put the plan in motion to have a French naval squadron trained for attacks on vessels to be sent to Syria.

As Friday 13 June 1941 dawned it was beginning to appear that the Vichy troops were continuing to fight with determination and that they showed no signs of cracking under the three-pronged assault. The Free French attack around Merjayoun had been a complete failure and the 5th Indian Brigade was now taking responsibility. The Australians had run into heavy defences on the coast. It was apparent now that the attacking forces under Wilson's control were woefully inadequate for the job. Consequently, Wavell authorized the deployment of the British 6th Division, but it would have to be moved up from Egypt.

The Vichy French Air Force was as active on 13 June as it had been before. GAO583 were, nonetheless, withdrawn from Rayak to re-establish at Baalbeck-la-Colonne. Pilot Officer Lea of 11 Squadron, flying a Blenheim on a photoreconnaissance mission over Beirut at around 1100 hours, was jumped by three Dewoitine 520s. The French spotted him at around 1130 hours and identified the aircraft as a Free French Martin. *Capitaine* Richard, followed by the other two Dewoitines, attacked. Lea tried to get away but Richard pressed home the attack. Riddled with bullets, Lea's aircraft crashed to the north of the Litani River; Lea and his crew were killed.

Four Morane 406s belonging to GCI/7 escorted four Loiré et Olivier LeO451s of GBI/31 in an attack on British cruisers off Sidon. The events that were to now take place could well explain some of the confusion regarding the engagement that Sergeant R.T. Wallace had reported taking place on 12 June. What apparently seems to have happened is that the French aircraft were attacked by an un-specified number of Hurricanes over Jezzine. One of the Morane 406 pilots, *Sous Lieutenant* Demoulin, incorrectly identified the Hurricanes as Tomahawks. What is clear is that the LeO451 flown by Lieutenant Lecerf was attacked by two aircraft. In the attack one of the gunners on board the LeO451, Sergeant de Feligonde, hit one of the Hurricanes and saw it break off, belching smoke. In the brief engagement de Feligonde was wounded. What this may mean is that the events that Wallace had noted down as taking place on 12 June actually happened on 13 June.

GBI/12 finally arrived in Syria during the course of the day. They had left France on 11 June, flying in via Brindisi. They had brought with them thirteen LeO451s and four Farman transports with equipment and ground crew. They landed at Aleppo, but on the following day they were transferred to Qousseir to join GBI/31 who had also been transferred there. GBI/31 had had a busy day on 13 June and the formation had flown three reconnaissance mission and twenty-one bombing sorties.

Saturday 14 June was the seventh day of the campaign. By the end of this first week the French had lost twelve aircraft in action and the British had lost nine. What was significant, however, was that the strength of the RAF had not increased over the course of the week. But the Vichy Air Force had grown considerably in strength.

There was still one day of fighting left in that first week and it began at 0627 hours, when five Blenheims belonging to 11 Squadron were launched in an attack on the airfield at Aleppo. Three of the Blenheims pounced on Rayak airfield, shooting up three Morane 406s on the ground. They came back for a second attack at 1330 hours, destroying a Morane 406 and writing off a Potez 25TOE.

The Vichy Government had also launched missions of their own early that morning. At 0500 hours *Sous Lieutenant* Collonfiers, in a Potez 63-11, had gone out on a reconnaissance mission along the coast. A stray shot from the ground hit his oil tank and he was forced to return to base. Collonfiers was part of GAO583. The unit had also sent out *Sous Lieutenant* Tatraux but he, too, came under ground fire, slightly damaging his aircraft as he carried out his reconnaissance over Kissoué.

Towards the end of the afternoon, at 1735 hours, GBI/31 launched five of their aircraft to attack the Royal Navy. This time they were accompanied by *Sous Lieutenant* Le Gloan, at the head of six

Dewoitine 520s. Shortly before 1730 hours Flying Officer, the Honourable David Coke, in a Hurricane of 80 Squadron, had been sent out on a reconnaissance mission over Beirut. He responded to the urgent call to make for the fleet to give them air cover. As he got there he could see four of the LeO451s dropping bombs on the Royal Navy vessels. Almost immediately he was attacked by three Vichy fighters. He was mistaken in the assumption that they were Morane 406s when, in fact, they were Dewoitine 520s. Coke sustained a few hits on the tail of his Hurricane but help was on its way.

Flying Officer P.T. Dowding arrived first and saw that Coke was on his own. Dowding immediately engaged one of the three Dewoitine 520s he could see. He opened fire on it and saw it dive away, belching smoke. Sergeant Hancock then arrived and came in to attack. For the next ten minutes Hancock was engaged in a dogfight with the Vichy fighters. At the end of the engagement Hancock was fairly certain he had shot one down. Dowding had had his kill confirmed by the Royal Navy, as they believed they had seen one of the Dewoitines crash into the sea. According to French records, this was not the case. The four Vichy pilots involved in the dogfight included Le Gloan, *Sergeant Chef* Mertzisen and *Sous Lieutenant* Brondel. The first two pilots got back to base, albeit with damage to their aircraft. Both of them claimed probable kills. Brondel was not so fortunate; his aircraft had been badly shot up and he had to make a forced landing, but the aircraft flipped over and was written off.

A little later, at 2000 hours, *Capitaine* Dessalles of GCI/7 led three Morane 406s to chase Blenheims that had attacked Aleppo. As Dessalles attacked one of the Blenheims, it fired back and he was forced to crash-land to the south-east of Nerab airfield.

The French continued to pour more aircraft into Syria. Commandant Lambert led seven LeO451s of GBI/25 into Aleppo. The ground crew and equipment were flown in by Air France D338s. The last Vichy Air Force units to arrive at the end of that first week actually did not make it until 15 June. These were twenty-one Dewoitine 520s belonging to GCII/3. They had flown in from Tunis, taking the long route to Brindisi then to Athens, on to Rhodes and finally to Homs.

Thus ended the first week of hostilities. For a short time the initiative would now turn to the Vichy French. There would be much more fighting on the ground and in the skies above Syria and Palestine, until Syria would be in Allied hands and all of the Vichy prisoners, except a handful that would opt to join the Free French, were shipped home to metropolitan France.

Chapter Five

Operation *Exporter* – Phase Two

By Saturday 14 June the British had driven a deep salient into Syria. The eastern thrust was south of Kissoué, which was just twenty-five miles from Damascus. Along the coast the British and Commonwealth forces were just thirty miles from Beirut. But in the Merjayoun region they were still only ten miles beyond the frontier. The Vichy French still held a strong defensive line, defending Damascus. They had good cover for infantry and tanks to the east of the Damascus road and the positions they held to the west of the road commanded the whole area.

On 14 June 1941 Brigadier Lloyd had taken over command of the Free French Gentforce, which had formerly been commanded by General Legentilhomme. The Free French general had been badly wounded when three Vichy Dewoitine 520s had strafed vehicles near Sanamein. The Frenchman had received a broken arm and flesh wounds. He was adamant that he should continue fighting after being patched up, but instead he was sent to the rear and Lloyd was put in temporary command.

Lloyd now planned for the Indian Brigade plus a battalion of Free French Marines to attack before dawn on 15 June. Their target was Kissoué. They hoped to catch the Vichy French unprepared. The Vichy forces were ready and prepared, however, and for four hours until 0830 hours there was hand-to-hand fighting amongst the orchards and gardens, with the brunt of the fighting being carried out by Punjabis. The Punjabis held onto the positions that they had dearly taken and Rajputs troops completed the assault on the dominant hill in the area, preceded by an artillery bombardment.

Meanwhile, Free French Marines and British Fusiliers cleared another village.

To begin with it all boded well, but the Vichy French were about to launch their own counter offensive. De Verdilhac had not committed the bulk of his Vichy troops. He had not committed his eighty or so tanks. He was still trying to wrestle with which of Wilson's attacks was the real one and not a feint. As a result, the Vichy command decided to hit as many places as possible, particularly to break up the attack on Damascus and to cut Wilson's fragile supply routes. The attacks were to bring about a major reversal for the British. The Vichy French spent Sunday 15 June 1941 moving troops up into position.

The 1st Royal Fusiliers were based around Kuneitra, with their forward company at Tel el Cham, sixteen miles to the north. The forward company were told to send out fighting patrols but not to become seriously engaged. At this tiny hamlet there were some Bren gun carriers, a pair of armoured cars of the Royal Dragoon Guards and a captured Italian 20 mm heavy machine gun. These men would be the first to discover that the French were manoeuvring to launch a major offensive.

At around 0230 hours Vichy French armoured cars, tanks and infantry began advancing from Sassa, about four miles from the position of the forward company. It was estimated that there were eleven tanks, ten armoured cars, two or more field guns and 1,500 infantry.

The forward company took to their Bren gun carriers and trucks, being covered by the Royal Dragoon Guards. By the time they got back to Kuneitra more than fifty of the men were missing; most of them had been captured. It was clear now that the Vichy French were not about to settle for having retaken a hamlet.

In the skies Flying Officer Macrostie of 208 Squadron in a Hurricane was on a reconnaissance mission. When he reached Kissoué, Allied anti-aircraft fire shot him down in error and he was killed. In the same area, at around daybreak, half a dozen Gladiators of X Flight, operating out of Mafraq, ran into a number of Dewoitine 520s led by *Sous Lieutenant* Le Gloan. The aircraft belonging to GCIII/6 spotted three of the Gladiators at around 0945 hours. Le Gloan, followed by *Capitaine* de Rivals-Mazères and *Sergeant Chef*

Mertzisen, shot down one of the Gladiators, killing Flight Officer J.N. Craigie. There was then a dogfight that ended in Mertzisen's Dewoitine being crippled and having to force land behind British lines at Sanamein. Le Gloan had attacked a second Gladiator, but had run out of ammunition. He was then chased by a pair of Gladiators. His aircraft was so badly damaged that he crash-landed it, writing it off at Rayak. *Sergeant Chef* Elmlinger and Sergeant Mequet also claimed a kill in the dogfight, but the only other Gladiator that was damaged in the battle was Pilot Officer Watson's aircraft, but he had managed to make it to Amman and land safely. Even though Mertzisen had landed behind British lines, Bedouins assisted him in getting back to Rayak by 20 June.

The job of protecting the 15th Cruiser Squadron had fallen to 80 Squadron during the day. They had intercepted nine German Ju88s from II/LG1 based in Crete, engaged in dive bombing. The Germans managed to hit HMS *Isis*. Six of 80 Squadron's Hurricanes tried to intercept the Ju88s. Flying Officer Dahl believed that he had shot down one of the bombers, but he was mistaken, as the Germans only lost one bomber and that one had been forced to crash-land in Turkey.

Lieutenant de V. Ziegler, at the head of *Aeronavale Escadrille* 6B, with Martin M167Fs, had only arrived on the morning of 15 June. They had taken off from Sidi Ahmed and had landed at Rayak. They were to fly their first mission at 1840 hours that night. Three of the bombers, accompanied by seven Dewoitine 520s of GCIII/6 and six Morane 406s of GCI/7, were tasked with bombing Royal Navy vessels. Also operating in the area was GBI/12 with four LeO451s. What is clear is that the destroyer HMS *Ilex*, which a pilot of 6B3 claimed to have sunk, was damaged. The Royal Navy believed that it had actually been hit by a Ju88. GBI/31 launched four more LeO451s at 1930 hours but they caused no damage to the Royal Navy vessels, although one of the Vichy aircraft was hit by anti-aircraft guns and damaged.

In the early evening seven Tomahawks of 3 RAAF Squadron were strafing Sheikh Meskine when they spotted five Martin M167Fs of GBI/39. The Martin flown by Lieutenant Baron was shot down and two of his crewmen were captured. They crash-landed near Deraa and were taken prisoner. *Sergeant Chef* Tanchoux's aircraft was also a victim; this time the pilot and his crew were all killed. The kills were claimed by Squadron Leader Jeffrey and Flying Officer Peter Turnbull.

As a result of these strong air attacks the 15th Cruiser Squadron withdrew toward Haifa. From now on it would only be used offensively at night and in the early morning, as long as it had air cover.

Toward the evening Flying Officer Holdsworth of A Flight, 208 Squadron, flew the same reconnaissance mission that Macrostie had flown the previous day when he had been shot down. Holdsworth suffered exactly the same fate as he, too, was shot down by Allied anti-aircraft fire. He managed to make a forced landing but Free French colonial troops mistakenly shot and killed him as he got out of his aircraft.

A Potez 63-11, flown by *Capitaine* Guignard of GRII/39, was shot down over Merjayoun at around 1745 hours, probably by anti-aircraft fire. The crewmembers were all killed. There was a significant attack against Deraa railway station during the night by Martins belonging to GBI/39 and Potez 25TOEs of *Groupement Faure*.

Monday 16 June saw a major Vichy French counterattack along the Damascus road. It was aimed at Kuneitra. The French had timed the attack extremely well, as they were now trying to target RAF airfields. Defending Kuneitra were the 1st Royal Fusiliers. The Vichy troops had begun moving at 0345 hours and by 0600 hours French tanks were roaming about the streets of Kuneitra. All that the British troops had to defend themselves with were about fifteen Boys anti-tank rifles. They had worked well against lightly armoured Italian tanks, but had proved to be completely useless against German tanks in France and were equally as ineffective against the French light Renault R-35 tanks belonging to the 7th *Chasseurs d'Afrique*, led by Colonel Lecoulteux. The Fusiliers had tried the anti-tank rifles, Molotov cocktails and grenades and, in desperation, had radioed for anti-tank guns to come up and deal with the French attack.

Major Bernard Fergusson, operating as the liaison officer to Gentforce, turned them down. They only had a handful of anti-tank guns and needed them for the attack on Damascus. As it was, for three or more hours, the Fusiliers continued to resist as best they could, but it was a forlorn hope. The French were making good use of the tanks, neutralizing any opposition. The tanks covered the Vichy infantry as they advanced house by house. The net result was inevitable, as Gavin Long reported in the official Australian history:

The siege started, the enemy sniping strongly from tanks and houses (wrote the historian of the Royal Fusiliers). Spirited replies from Bren gunners reduced the numbers of enemy snipers ... the tanks roamed exactly where they liked and cruised round the battalion area shooting up the trenches, into doors and windows and at all trucks ... Tank-hunting squads, mostly M.T. drivers, drew grenades from the battalion reserve S.A.A. truck ... and continued their hopeless hunt ... At about this time Corporal Cotton, D.C.M., distinguished himself for the last time. He withdrew to the area of battalion headquarters at about 1230 hours. With Second Lieutenant Connal and one Fusilier, he carried back a Hotchkiss machine-gun he had captured a week before, together with 1,300 rounds. With this he continued in action for half an hour, but when the gun broke down he took an anti-tank rifle and went to attack the tanks single-handed. He drew their fire and was eventually killed by a round of high-explosive ... There were many other gallant deeds that day. Towards the evening it looked as if the enemy infantry had withdrawn, as there was a lull. At 1820 hours a French officer approached in an armoured car, waving a white handkerchief, and came to battalion headquarters with a Fusilier prisoner. The officer explained that the battalion was surrounded by a vastly superior force of tanks and other armoured fighting vehicles. He hoped they would surrender now, as he hated shooting Englishmen. The Commanding Officer demanded half an hour to decide. After consultation with the second-in-command and Regimental Sergeant-Major, he decided that to give in was the only alternative to the massacre of the remainder of his men ... As he went over to speak to the French Commander, he saw eleven medium tanks behind the nearest group of houses. At 1900 hours he surrendered, with thirteen officers and 164 other ranks.

This was not the only disaster; the 6th *Chasseurs d'Afrique* had stormed Merjayoun with their Renault R-35s. This time there were anti-tank units and three of the French tanks were knocked out. But despite the heroics of Australians and British Scots Greys, operating as motorized infantry, the town fell and the Vichy French were now just an hour's drive from the Palestinian border. The French had bypassed the bulk of the 25th Australian Brigade, which had stormed Jezzine, but now this also came under attack.

In the early hours of 16 June 1941 three of 11 Squadron's Blenheims attacked Rayak. Gladiators of X Flight, along with Tomahawks of 3 RAAF Squadron, began aggressive patrols.

In support of the ground effort four LeO451s belonging to GBI/12 and GBI/31, escorted by Morane 406s, hit British targets around Jezzine. At the same time a number of British aircraft were spotted on landing strip H4. As a result, the GBI/12 launched five of their aircraft, supported by three belonging to GBI/31, to attack at 1325 hours. They bombed an unoccupied landing strip some way to the east of H4 by mistake.

On the previous day a Sunderland of 230 Squadron, based at Alexandria, had spotted the *Guepard*, *Chevalier Paul* and *Valmy*, three French destroyers, *en route* from Toulon to Syria. Swordfish of 815 Squadron, operating out of Cyprus, attacked them, with Sub-Lieutenant Day hitting the *Chevalier Paul* with a torpedo. Three Gladiators also came in to attack but the aircraft crewed by Lieutenant M.G.W. Clifford and Sub-Lieutenant Winter was shot down and they were captured by the Vichy French. The *Chevalier Paul* was sunk but the majority of her crew were picked up by the other two French destroyers.

In the nick of time Operation *Battleaxe*, which had been an attempt to end the siege of Tobruk, was cancelled after two days. Although the operation was a failure, it meant that Wavell could now afford to send some of his carefully husbanded infantry reserves to Syria. One of the first units to arrive was the 2nd Queen's. They would be able to recapture Kuneitra at bayonet point, supported by a single 25-pdr gun. It cost them just one casualty. The Vichy French had decided not to risk losing their precious tanks on a determined dash and face the prospect of losing them all if they got cut off without access to fuel. Although the initiative was now switching back towards Wilson and his forces, there was still a great deal to be achieved, not the least of which was to regain ground that the Vichy French had taken back.

It was the French, however, that got in the first blows on 17 June 1941, with seven LeO415s of GBI/12 and GBI/31 leaving Quosseir to bomb enemy targets around Merjayoun at 0935 hours. The newly arrived GCII/3 Dewoitine 520s were on escort duty. These nine aircraft were making their first Syrian sorties. Three Martins of *Escadrille* 6B made an attack on a British battery near Jezzine in the afternoon, whilst another one of their Martins buzzed over Cyprus on a reconnaissance mission. Five LeO415s of GBI/25 attacked targets to the south of Damascus and four others raided targets near Qatana. GBI/25 moved to Homs as their new operational base that evening.

At around 1835 hours Kissoué came under attack and a bridge at Oauaj, over the River Nar, was attacked by ten LeO451s belonging to GBI/12 and GBI/31. The Potez 63-11 piloted by *Capitaine* Capdaspe-Couchet of GRII/39 was shot down on a reconnaissance over Kissoué. There is dispute as to whether the aircraft was hit by anti-aircraft fire, or by Hurricanes of 80 Squadron. Capdaspe-Couchet died of his wounds that night and the other two crew-members were wounded. All three of the men had found themselves in enemy hands.

Seven more Martin 167Fs arrived from Sidi Ahmed. They had left their base on 14 June, flying first to Brindisi then to Athens. From there they had flown to Rayak and joined *Escadrille* 6B at Madjaloun.

In order for the whole invasion plan not to become an unmitigated and drawn out disaster, the British instituted a number of changes on 18 June. By this stage Ezraa and Kuneitra had both been retaken, but Merjayoun was still in Vichy French hands. General Blamey became Deputy Commander in Chief of the Middle East; General Lavarack of the 1st Australian Corps took over command of all land units. Command of the 7th Australian Division was given to Major General A.S. Allen and Major General J.F. Evetts, who was commander of the British 6th Division, took direct command of troops, excluding the Free French around the Damascus, Deraa and Kuneitra region.

For a time the fighting on the ground concentrated around the Mezze airfield. A major attempt was made on 18 June to capture it. In fact, the operation had got underway at 2030 hours the previous day. Punjabi troops had caught a number of Renault R-35 tank crews unprepared. They had scattered the crews and destroyed several of the tanks. The Vichy French quickly recovered and the Punjabis had to storm their positions. Despite the heavy casualties, the airfield was reached at 0415 hours on 18 June. Once again, the French had been caught napping and all the lights were on. After an hour's fighting the village and the airfield were in British hands.

The French now launched a counter-attack, firstly to dislodge the Indian troops that had set up a road block on the Beirut road. The Vichy attack was spearheaded by Renault R-35 tanks. The Indian troops began falling back, believing that they were simply drawing the enemy tanks into an ambush where they would be blown to pieces by anti-tank guns. It quickly began to take on the same features that had faced the Royal Fusiliers; there were no anti-tank guns and all the Indians had to fight them off with was a single Boys anti-tank rifle. Some of the Indians found themselves cut off and were forced to surrender when Vichy tanks began firing at the building at point-blank range. But this was not to be Kuneitra all over again; there would be no surrender. The Indians began making Molotov cocktails. Had the French watched them pour wine down the sink and replace it with petrol they would have been mortified.

The French tanks were supported by Senegalese troops and as darkness began to fall the Indians had already beaten back a determined Senegalese attack with Bren guns, grenades and then a bayonet charge. They had also destroyed at least one of the Renault tanks. So far there was no sign of the rest of their brigade.

The main defensive position was around Mezze house, which had formerly been the home of the British representative of the Iraqi Petroleum Company. It was a brilliant position, as it had running water, a tall wall around it, high-ceilinged rooms, shuttered windows and an ample supply of canned petrol in the garage. This was in addition to the oil man's collection of wine in the cellar. Inside were around 250 men, largely of the 3/1 Punjabis and the 4th Rajputan Rifles, all under the command of Colonel Lionel Jones. They also had with them some fifty French prisoners of war.

As it got dark three of the men crept out through a hole in the wall, trying to make for the British lines. It took them all night and they did not arrive until 0530 hours the following morning. It was then that they realized exactly what had gone wrong and why they had not been more closely supported by the rest of the brigade.

The Free French were commanded by Colonel Magrin-Vernet, a former French Foreign Legion man who had adopted the name of Monclar. He had actually resigned his role as infantry commander owing to the fact that he would not fight against some of his old comrades belonging to the 6th Foreign Legion. As a result, the French infantry had remained in Kissoué.

Legentilhomme resumed command of Gentforce, whilst Lloyd took back command of what remained of the 5th Indian Brigade. They despatched Major Patrick Bourk with two companies of Punjabis and one company of Fusiliers. He also had with him twelve 25-pdr guns. The troops inside Mezze house had come under fire at dawn. The Vichy French were rather reluctant to get too close to the house with their tanks for fear of the volleys of Molotov cocktails being thrown in their direction. By around midday the defenders of the house could clearly hear different noises; there was distant small arms fire and the heavy boom of artillery.

De Verdilhac threw more troops in to try and overwhelm Mezze house but more British reinforcements were on their way. Lieutenant Colonel David Lamb's Australian 2/3 Battalion had arrived and Vichy troops had begun to fall back. They made one more attempt to try and overwhelm Mezze house by bringing up a pair of 75 mm field guns. They fired at close range and one of the shells wrecked the roof above one of the rooms where wounded were being kept. They also managed to smash a hole in the garden wall, through which Senegalese troops began to pour.

Captain John Robertson, a former tea planter who had been wounded at Sidi Barrani, was leading his Punjabis and launched a counter-attack. He emptied his revolver into the leading Senegalese and then, at the head of his men, drove the Senegalese out at the point of a bayonet.

What remained of the men inside Mezze house now realized that help could not be very far away and tried to play for time by asking the Vichy for a truce. The Senegalese, choosing to ignore the white flag, charged in and shot two of the Rajputs. It was only the intervention of a French officer that prevented the remnants of the garrison from being slaughtered.

Four hours later the British had broken through to Mezze House. One side of the house had collapsed and there were over 100 bodies inside the building. Just outside the garden were three gutted Vichy tanks. An Indian medical officer was later found in a hospital; he had stayed behind with the wounded and he was able to confirm that the defenders of Mezze House had not actually surrendered but had been literally overrun.

Although it had ended in failure, as far as breaking through to Mezze house before they were overwhelmed, it had, in fact, been the turning point of the battle for Damascus. The vast majority of de Verdilhac's men had been sucked into the fight. It meant that that night the road to Beirut was well and truly cut. De Verdilhac's men headed towards Homs in the north. It would not be long before Damascus would fall.

While the events on the ground were taking place the air war between 18 June and the final abandonment of Damascus on 21 June by Vichy troops was primarily focused on the Mezze area.

At 0400 hours on 18 June 1941 four Potez 25TOEs of EO596 bombed vehicles to the south-east of Abu Kemal. Nearly five hours later a single Potez 63-11 of GOA583 was accompanied by no fewer than seven Dewoitine 520s of GCIII/6. Leading the Dewoitines was *Capitaine* Rivals-Mazères, but he had to turn back as a result of engine difficulties. Le Gloan took over and dived down to attack British vehicles near Kissoué. In the area were five out of six X Flight Gladiators. One had had to head home due to engine problems. The Gladiators were led by Flying Officer Young and they were at a greater altitude than the French fighters. The Gladiators pounced, shooting down Lieutenant Boiries and then took out a second Dewoitine. This left three Vichy aircraft against five Gladiators, as Le Gloan was investigating ground targets. The Dewoitines broke off, having inflicted no damage on the Gladiators at all.

At around 1335 hours vehicles on the road near Merjayoun came under attack from nine LeO451s of GBI/12 and GBI/31. They had an escort of nine Dewoitine 520s of GCII/3. Just under two hours later eleven Martin M167Fs of *Flotille* 4F, led by *Capitaine* Huber, attacked Jezzine.

GCIII/6, after many days of combat, was now down to eight serviceable aircraft. But on 19 June five new aircraft and crew arrived. By recent standards 19 June was comparatively quiet; there were a number of reconnaissance flights flown and one of the major attacks launched by the Vichy French took place at 1605 hours. This was when the first five of ten Martins belonging to *Flotille* 4F attacked Australian positions around Sidon. Seven Tomahawks of 3 RAAF Squadron made for the Sidon area. They attacked Martins belonging to both *Escadrilles* 6B and 7B. They inflicted some damage on the bombers but the Tomahawks had to break off, largely due to the fact that they were virtually out of fuel.

To put things into perspective, this was the evening when the lead Indian units had taken Mezze airfield, only to find themselves isolated. By Friday 20 June the RAF could content themselves with making numerous attacks on French troops that were falling back to Beirut. This meant that the Vichy French had to reply in kind by focusing its attention on this area.

Nine LeO415s attacked positions to the south-east of Damascus in the afternoon, the aircraft being supplied by GBI/12 and GBI/31. They were protected by eleven Dewoitine 520s of GCII/3. Later on that day five of the bombers returned, escorted by Morane 406s of GCI/7. A Martin M167F of GBI/39 was shot down by anti-aircraft fire over Jezzine that day. The pilot, Lieutenant Ancel, and the observer, Lieutenant Duparchy, were both killed, as was a third member of the crew. The remaining crewmember was captured by British forces.

A French reconnaissance flight over Iraq discovered a convoy of 800 or more vehicles moving towards Palmyra and Abu Kemal; this was *Habforce*.

Habforce had remained in the Habbaniya area since the armistice in Iraq. It was now decided that the force would be used against Syria. Consequently, the organization of *Habforce* was to now include:

- 4th Cavalry Brigade – consisting of the Household Cavalry Regiment, the Royal Wiltshire Yeomanry and the Warwickshire Yeomanry.

- 1st Battalion of the Essex Regiment.
- 237th Battery of the 60 Field Regiment Royal Artillery (with 25 pdrs).
- A battery of Australian 2-pdr anti-tank guns.
- 169th Light Anti-Aircraft Battery.
- Arab Legion Mechanized Regiment – which now consisted of 350 men organized into a headquarters unit and nine troops of motorized infantry, along with a troop of three home-made armoured cars.

It was decided that the force should be split into three columns for their advance on Palmyra. The Royal Wiltshires were to pass Palmyra to the south and west, along with a detachment from the Arab legion. The rest of the 4th Cavalry Brigade would pass to the east, again guided by a detachment from the Arab legion. The remaining force was probably the one that was spotted by the Vichy French, as this was the column that moved off on the morning of 21 June 1941.

An attack had to be made on pillboxes and an isolated fort some forty miles from Palmyra. This had given the Vichy sufficient warning that the force was on its way. In fact, on 21 June *Capitaine* Tonon of GBI/12, in a LeO451, spotted 150 vehicles or more approaching Palmyra. Two hours or so later four LeO451s raided the column and six more attacked later on that afternoon. Attacks were also launched by nine Morane 406s. At this stage they would have probably been from GCI/7. Additional attacks were made by GCII/3. They made twenty-six sorties during the day. Potez 25TOEs were launched to make night attacks.

Sitting in Palmyra were a pair of French Foreign Legion companies and a light desert company. But Palmyra was clearly under immediate threat.

Meanwhile, on the coast, having spotted a number of Royal Navy warships not far off Beirut, nine Martin M167Fs of *Flotille* 4F came in to attack. At the same time Vichy fighters belonging to GCI/7 and GCII/3 were protecting the Vichy destroyer *Vauqelin*, which had made the long journey from southern France. Also, the first of a number of new Martins belonging to GRI/22 arrived at Madjaloun.

On Sunday 22 June 1941, 4,500,000 German troops and their allies, supported by 600,000 vehicles, 750,000 horses and nearly

4,500 aircraft, invaded Russia. It had been a long planned operation, which to some extent had been fortuitously delayed by the
Germans' need to assist the Italians in the war that they were losing
against the Greeks. Vital German military resources had been drawn
into the conflict, much against Hitler's better judgement. Subse-
quent to this, air assets were being bled away by operations that
would culminate in the capture of Crete and then, to a lesser extent
in the support of the failed Iraqi revolt against the British and then
an attempt to support the Vichy French in Syria and Palestine.

Meanwhile, on the ground around Palmyra, the modest Vichy
French Air Force had turned virtually its entire attention on the
growing threat of *Habforce*. Continued air attacks had brought the
columns almost to a standstill within twenty-five miles of Palmyra.
The ground units were losing precious vehicles and they had very
little to fight back with, lacking a great deal of anti-aircraft weapons.
They did, however, manage to shoot down a Potez 63-11 belonging
to GAO583. But there were raids by Martins throughout the day and
towards the end of the afternoon a Morane 406 flown by *Sous
Lieutenant* Seinturier of GCI/7 was also shot down, the pilot being
killed.

The Vichy French could not afford to throw absolutely everything
against *Habforce*, although they managed to launch around 120
sorties throughout the course of 22 June. The Vichy held back
GCIII/6 to provide protection for Beirut harbour and GRII/39
focused on the Damascus region.

The British, however, were not put off in their attempts to destroy
the newly arrived French destroyer. Led by Flying Officer R.H.
Moore, three Blenheims of 11 Squadron attempted to sink her. They
managed to achieve six hits, killing five of the sailors. Moore's
aircraft was badly shot up in the attack and his observer, Sergeant
Manley, was badly wounded.

To a large extent, Monday 23 June saw the beginning of the last
phase of the campaign. On almost every front barring Palmyra,
Vichy troops were in retreat. In addition to this, more British aircraft
were being pulled out of Egypt and brought up to take part in the
Syrian campaign, in a last desperate attempt to overwhelm the
Vichy. A section of Hurricanes belonging to 33 Squadron joined
806 Squadron based at Lydda. At the same time, additional men

from 450 RAAF Squadron had been brought up to join 260 Squadron and 80 Squadron. These men, effectively a composite unit, came under the command of Squadron Leader C.J. Mount, DFC. The RAF considered that the most important mission should be to try to destroy as many Vichy aircraft as possible. This would be the only way that they could take pressure off *Habforce*.

At around 1320 hours on 23 June ten Hurricanes, six belonging to 80 Squadron and four from the newly formed 260/450 Squadron, struck Merjayoun. They were then to attack Baalbeck and Rayak. The attack got off to a good start when they shot up an abandoned Martin M167F at Merjayoun. They then swooped in on Baalbeck and caught five more Martins that had only just landed. The Martins were from GBI/39 and one of them burst into flames; the second one blew up. They badly damaged a third plane. They also caught four Martins that were about to take off, belonging to *Flotille* 4F, scoring hits on all of them. Two Potez 63-11s, belonging to GRII/39, were also destroyed in this attack, with a third being so badly damaged that it had to be written off, as did in all probability a fourth Potez. They also smashed up and destroyed a Potez 25TOE of EO593, badly damaged a Potez 63-11 belonging to GAO583 and caused some damage to a Farman 222-1 belonging to GTI/15.

Scrambling to deal with the attack were Dewoitine 520s of GCIII/6 at Rayak. Four of the aircraft got aloft in time for the first part of the dogfight. These were *Sous Lieutenant* Le Gloan, *Capitaine* Richard, *Sergeant Chef* Mertzisen and Sergeant Coisneau. Le Gloan claimed to have shot one of the Hurricanes down and the other three pilots claimed a second between them. More Dewoitines arrived and Lieutenant Stenou claimed to have shot down another Hurricane and a second shared with the newly arrived on the scene, *Sergeant Chef* Maccia and *Sous Lieutenant* Satgé. In fact, 260/450 Squadron lost three Hurricanes in the engagement; Pilot Officer T. Livingstone was wounded, Sergeant G.J. Black baled out and was taken prisoner and Pilot Officer Baldwin was killed. The French also shot up the Hurricane belonging to Pilot Officer O.V. Hanbury.

As far as the Vichy French losses are concerned in the engagement, once again there is some dispute. Although confused, it does appear that Sergeant Michaux's aircraft was badly damaged and he was forced to crash-land. A little later, at 1455 hours, *Sergeant Chef* Monribot and Sergeant Coisneau, also of GCIII/6, reported attacking a Hurricane just off the coast, at Damour. They then claimed that they had shot it down and had seen a parachute. In fact, it was not a Hurricane at all, but a 45 Squadron Blenheim being flown by Pilot Officer Champion on a Beirut reconnaissance mission. The Blenheim did sustain enough damage for it to crash on landing. In all likelihood, what the two Vichy pilots had seen was Pilot Officer Livingstone's parachute.

Qousseir came under attack from twelve Tomahawk aircraft of 3 RAAF Squadron at 1720 hours that day. They destroyed a LeO451 belonging to GBI/31, although the aircraft had already been abandoned.

The Dewoitines of GCIII/6 were aloft again at 1834 hours. Nine of them were pounced on by the Tomahawks that had attacked the airfield just over an hour before. In the engagement *Sous Lieutenant* Le Gloan's aircraft was hit several times and began to burn, so he made off as quickly as possible. Lieutenant Stenou and Sergeant Savinel were both shot down by Flying Officer Bothwell and both the Vichy French pilots were killed. A pair of the Tomahawks was also damaged in this engagement.

A number of Morane 406s of GCI/7, which were now at the Nerab airfield at Aleppo, strafed vehicles near pumping station T3. This station was part of *Habforce*.

The Hurricanes of 80 Squadron and 260/450 hit the airfields at Baalbeck at around noon on 24 June. They claimed to have seen over twenty bombers and to have shot several of them up. But, in fact, they only managed to damage GTI/15's pair of Farman 222.1s. The two transport aircraft were very badly damaged and were soon written off.

As far as the Vichy French was concerned, the focus of the attacks on 24 June was once again Habforce, with LeO451s of GBI/12 and GBI/31, along with GBI/25 mustering fifteen sorties between them. The aircraft flown by *Sous Lieutenant* Lerat was shot down by anti-aircraft fire and crash-landed, killing all of the crewmembers. Led by Lieutenant de V. Ziegler, seven *Aéronavale* Martin M167Fs made an evening attack on *Habforce*, to the south-east of Palmyra.

The RAF finally gave *Habforce* some air cover on 25 June, in the shape of eight Tomahawks from 3 RAAF Squadron. They took off from H4 at around 1330 hours and were just in time to intercept six LeO451s, which were evenly split, three each from GBI/12 and GBI/31. As far as the GBI/12 aircraft were concerned it was to be an absolute disaster, as none of their three aircraft would return. The majority of the Vichy French crewmembers were killed.

If 25 June had been a disaster for the Vichy forces then 26 June was to be even worse. The day began badly, when *Capitaine* Bordier and *Capitaine* Menu, in Dewoitine 520s of GCII/3, were on a reconnaissance mission at 0600 hours. Bordier's aircraft was shot down by anti-aircraft fire and he was killed.

Then began the major reversal of the week; coming in from H4 to attack Homs airfield were nine Australian Tomahawks. They had caught the bulk of GCII/3 on the ground, parked a little too close for comfort. In the space of ten seconds five of the Dewoitine 520s were ablaze, six were very badly damaged and eleven more were riddled with bullet holes. Not content with that, they then swept on to Rayak, where they destroyed another Dewoitine 520, damaged two more and destroyed three Potez 25TOEs and put holes in another two. But they were not finished for the day. They then fell on some Vichy motor transport and shot it up. Sergeant Baillie's aircraft was hit by anti-aircraft fire but he managed to nurse his aircraft to make a forced landing in Palestine, just north of the Sea of Galilee.

Rayak came under attack once again that evening when twelve Hurricanes, six each from 80 Squadron and 260/450 Squadron, strafed parked aircraft. They claimed to have destroyed three Dewoitines and a Potez 63, but, in fact, all of the serviceable Vichy aircraft had already been withdrawn to Nerab and, undoubtedly, the Hurricanes had simply shot up partially destroyed or unserviceable aircraft.

The LeO451s were again in action on 26 June, mounting fifteen sorties against *Habforce*. But by now it was becoming clear that the British were winning the air war and that the stretched resources of the Vichy French were coming under much greater strain. Undoubtedly, it would soon snap.

Friday 27 June 1941 saw the end of the third week of the campaign. Vichy French activity was reduced to just forty-five sorties overall. Nonetheless, they still managed to mount attacks on the Royal Navy. In this third week of the war the French had lost twenty-four aircraft for the cost of three Hurricanes and a pair of Tomahawks. There was still significant numbers of French aircraft still in Syria, however, including twenty-three serviceable Dewoitine 520s.

Nine Tomahawks of 3 RAAF Squadron were fortuitously aloft, having flown up to Mezze to refuel and then, at 1015 hours, were accompanying Blenheims on a raid. Five minutes earlier, *Flotille* 4F had launched six Martin M167Fs to attack *Habforce*. The Blenheims, having achieved their mission, had turned for home, but the Tomahawk pilots noticed bombing and sped to investigate. In the next few minutes every single French bomber was shot down, largely with total loss of life. Of all of the crewmembers, six officers and fourteen men were killed. Sergeant Wilson had claimed one, Flying Officer Turnbull two and Flight Lieutenant A.C. Rawlinson three. The Tomahawks had not lost a single aircraft in the combat, but on the return flight to Jenin the Tomahawk flown by Sergeant Randall cut out and he was killed when it crashed.

It had been the casualties inflicted on the Vichy French fighters that were proving to be the tipping point in the war. GCII/3 and GCIII/6 were now operating together. Six of these aircraft strafed the Palmyra area and the remaining LeO451s launched twenty-one sorties against *Habforce* on 28 June 1941.

There was more bad news for the Vichy on 29 June, which began ominously with the loss of *Sous Lieutenant* Pouey and his crew of their Potez 63-11 of GAO583 to anti-aircraft fire. The French also lost a Morane 406 when Adjutant Dufour was killed as it crash-landed. Seven LeO451s of GBI/25 bombed the Palmyra area, escorted by three Dewoitine 520s of GCII/3 and three more from GCIII/6 at around noon.

The Vichy forces now decided to shift the Martins belonging to GBI/39 from Madjaloun to Qousseir. The move was made towards the end of daylight hours, but barely an hour after they had arrived at Qousseir, 3 RAAF Squadron swooped in. Eight of their Tomahawks destroyed three of the bombers. They badly shot up a fourth bomber and also damaged a Farman and a transport aircraft. Infrastructure damage was also heavy, with a fuel storage tank, a hangar and ammunition store all going up in flames. This was not the only punishment meted out by the Tomahawks; inbound was *Sous Lieutenant* Lefroid in his Martin. He had just dropped off medical supplies. Flying Officer Arthur and Flying Officer Knowles chased the Martin for half an hour and shot it down off the coast of Beirut. None of the Vichy French crew survived.

At 0450 hours on 30 June 1941 Commandant Lambert, at the head of seven LeO451s of GBI/21, escorted by six Dewoitines of GCIII/6, attacked *Habforce*. They returned seven hours later; this time escorted by seven Dewoitines.

Meanwhile, operating out of Mosul, 84 Squadron's Blenheims raided the airfields at Aleppo on three occasions that day. The only probable damage was to an Air France D338, which was destroyed. Madjaloun was hit by ten Hurricanes belonging to 260/450 Squadron. They managed to shoot up a couple of *Aéronavale* aircraft and destroy an already damaged Martin.

By 1 July, attacks against *Habforce* would be even more hazardous for the Vichy forces than before. Advance units of 127 Squadron, consisting of four Hurricanes and four Gladiators, had been moved up from Haditha to pumping station T1. Equally, a whole brigade from the 10th Indian Division was edging towards Aleppo. On the same day, at around 0730 hours, Glubb's Arab Legion was on a reconnaissance sweep to the north-west, close to Aleppo. They had checked out a Christian village, As-Sukhna, which was believed to have been the base for Vichy raiders, which were causing considerable problems along *Habforce*'s supply lines. All they found, however, was a deserted French police post.

Suddenly, through his field glasses, Glubb saw vehicle dust. On closer inspection, he saw white flags and tricolours adorning six armoured cars and four trucks. Glubb had thirty men and three homemade armoured cars with him. He had sent the rest of his men into a valley to the rear to collect firewood, in order to make breakfast. Glubb watched from a ridge as the French column halted around 500m from him. He watched the Frenchmen get out of their vehicles and lay down, and knew they had made a terrible mistake. Glubb detailed his armoured cars and thirty men to hold the ridge while he rushed to call up his machinegun trucks, which could then launch a flank attack and surround the enemy. However by the time

Glubb got back to the scene with the trucks the armoured cars and the thirty men had overrun the French on their own. What remained of the French were running.

What followed next was a 60 mph chase across the desert, with the Vichy 2nd Light Desert Company being chased by Glubb's Bedouins. The French knew that the Bedouins were not known for taking prisoners. The chase continued until the French were cornered in a box valley. Glubb moved forward to accept the French surrender. One of the French officers committed suicide, but the rest of them, three French officers and eighty Syrians, surrendered. All of the armoured cars, trucks and heavy equipment were captured for the loss of one killed and one wounded. From then on, there would be no more raids on *Habforce*'s supply lines.

The Australian Tomahawks were hard at work again on 1 July 1941, pouncing on Baalbeck, where they shot up several Potez 63-11s and Potez 25TOEs. At least one of the former was irreparably damaged and two of the latter destroyed. The Vichy GBI/25 launched more raids on the Palmyra area that day, whilst other LeO451s from different groups attacked moving vehicles in the same area. Four of 127 Squadron's Hurricanes encountered three Dewoitine 520s of GCII/3 shortly after 1600 hours. They badly damaged *Sergeant Chef* Killy's aircraft, wounding him and forcing him to crash-land when he limped back to Aleppo. Shortly afterwards, having landed, the aircraft flown by Commandant Morlot burst into flames on the ground as a result of the damage that had been inflicted on it during the dogfight.

For some time the French had been trying to negotiate with the Germans to allow them to send ground troops to reinforce Syria. Initially, they had hoped that the Germans would cooperate in helping to transport French infantry using German aircraft. But it quickly became clear that the only way to transport the troops would be by sea. A battalion had already reached Thessaloniki but the Turks had refused to allow the battalion to transit through their country. As a result, the battalion clambered aboard a pair of transports, the *Oued-Yquem* and the *Saint-Didier*. French naval vessels steamed out of Beirut to help guide them in. But it was not going to be an easy journey.

By 2 July the Indian 10th Division was in place. The 17th Brigade was positioned in the north-east corner of Syria, guarding the railway line. The 21 Brigade Group moved up to Abu Kemal and the 20th Indian Infantry Brigade headed for Mosul.

The Vichy garrison at Palmyra, along with the outpost at T3 pumping station, surrendered on 2 July. There were just 187 men left. There were six French officers, forty-eight air force ground crew and eighty-seven Foreign Legionnaires. There were also fourteen Syrians. Despite the surrender, the Vichy had fought extremely well and had stubbornly held up 3,000 British troops for twelve days.

Also on the same day, four Blenheims of 84 Squadron hit Abu Danne, the home of GBI/12 and GBI/31. By the time the raid was over the two groups had four aircraft left between them. At roughly the same time Hurricanes of 127 Squadron were also aloft, as were six Dewoitine 520s from GCII/3 and four from GCIII/6. The Vichy fighters had been escorting three LeO451s of GBI/25 on a bombing mission to Palmyra. Three Dewoitines, flown by Sergeant Hurtin, Lieutenant Patin and *Adjutant Chef* Le Blanc, attacked the Hurricanes. Patin peeled off to deal with the Blenheims and managed to shoot two of them down. Flight Lieutenant Williams and his crew force-landed and were taken prisoner and Sergeant Batch's aircraft also had to make a forced landing.

3 July saw the end of the fourth week of operations but there was at least one more dramatic air engagement before the week would be out. The French were desperately trying to protect their troops that were holding out at Deir ez Zor and at 0930 hours four LeO451s from GBI/12 and GBI/31 attacked vehicles whilst being escorted by nine Dewoitine 520s.

Later, at 1250 hours, Hama airfield was attacked by ten Hurricanes belonging to 260/450 Squadron; this was now the main base for GBI/25. Two of the LeO451s were destroyed, two damaged beyond repair and six others were shot up.

The major engagement of the day was over Deir ez Zor. Three LeO451s of GBI/12 were being escorted on another mission by five Dewoitines of GCII/3 and three more of GCIII/6. A pair of Hurricanes on patrol over the area, belonging to 127 Squadron, came in to attack one of the bombers. Lieutenant Legrand, *Sergeant Chef* Maccia and Sergeant Ghesquière of GCIII/6 collectively shot down Flight

Sergeant Adams' Hurricane. Warrant Officer Pitcher was piloting the other Hurricane. His aircraft was riddled with bullets from one of the bombers, but it then collided with Lieutenant Bardollet's LeO451. Both of the Hurricanes had been lost, but Bardollet managed to nurse his damaged machine back to base.

The week's operations ended with the British having lost just four aircraft and the Vichy French twenty-one of theirs. This now meant that collectively GCII/3 and GCIII/6 had twenty-three Dewoitines left. There were thirteen Morane 406s with GCI/7 and thirty LeO451s, nine Martin M167Fs and five Potez 63-11s.

On 4 July some reinforcements arrived for the Vichy French in the shape of half a dozen Morane 406s, although, in fact, only four managed to make it to Rayak. One had crash-landed at Rome and another had proved to be unserviceable at Athens. No sooner had they arrived at Aleppo than one of them caught fire, killing Adjutant Chef Landry. A dozen *Aéronavale* Dewoitine 520s, led by Lieutenant de V. Pirel arrived from Morocco and, in addition, six open-cockpit seaplanes, used as torpedo bombers, the Late 298 float planes, flew into the Lebanese port of Tripoli. Another five Dewoitine 520s also arrived at Aleppo, which were shared out between GCIII/6 and GCII/3.

There were two encounters for Blenheims over the Aleppo area on 4 July 1941, the first of which involved a Blenheim from 45 Squadron being chased by three Morane 406s, but he managed to escape. The second one, belonging to 84 Squadron and flown by Pilot Officer Ryan, was less lucky. *Adjutant Chef* Amarger and *Sous Lieutenant* Fabre, also in Moranes, intercepted Ryan. Amarger hit the left engine and continued to fire. Ryan was wounded but managed to bale out before his aircraft crashed, killing the rest of his crew. Ryan was taken prisoner. The British also launched raids on Hama, Baalbeck and Madjaloun, but all these managed to achieve was to shoot up already badly damaged aircraft. The remaining LeO451s launched fourteen sorties on 4 July against the Deir ez Zor area. In one of the attacks, in the afternoon, *Sous Lieutenant* Laurent's aircraft of GBI/12 was hit by anti-aircraft fire. The crew baled out and were handed over to the British.

By now, the first of the French troop ships had crept down the Turkish coastline and had reached the Gulf of Adalia. The steamer

Saint-Didier was attacked at 0700 hours on 4 July by a Fleet Air Arm Albacore belonging to 829 Squadron out of Cyprus. The torpedoes narrowly missed her. Another attack was made at 1250 hours, which again ended in failure. Three more attempts to sink the ship were made before 1400 hours; each time the helmsman was sufficiently proficient to dodge the torpedoes. Towards the late afternoon the vessel had anchored around 400 yards off the port of Adalia. The idea was to try to make a dash down the coast as far as Latakia under cover of darkness. Precisely why the French thought that the British would observe Turkish territorial integrity cannot be explained, as they certainly were not doing it by attempting to sneak down the Turkish coast. Four Albacores came in at around 1700 hours. The first torpedo missed the ship and blew a hole in the breakwater of the port. This would lead to the Turks lodging a diplomatic protest. The other three torpedoes smashed into the vessel and she sank with the loss of fifty-two, with eighteen more being injured. Around 500 others on board survived and were interned by the Turks. As a result of this failure the other troop ship, *Oued-Yquem*, made for Rhodes, where it arrived four days later.

By 5 July the 21st Brigade of the 10th Indian Division was threatening Aleppo and the airfields. The major aerial combat of the day took place over Deir ez Zor. Air cover was provided by 127 Squadron. In the same area were around twelve Dewoitine 520s, covering bombing attacks by LeO451s. Once again, there would be a confusing dogfight, with contradictory claims. What becomes clear is that all the British had aloft at the time was a Gladiator and two Hurricanes, which were being flown by Squadron Leader Bodman and Flight Lieutenant Cremin. *Sous Lieutenant* Le Gloan and *Sergeant Chef* Mertzisen shot down Bodman's aircraft to the north-east. Meanwhile, *Capitaine* Richard and *Sergeant Chef* Loi chased the other one. They were joined by Le Gloan. Between them, they also managed to shoot down Cremin. Both of the RAF pilots survived.

The 7th Australian Division was preparing for an offensive, which they launched at midnight on 5 to 6 July. They crossed the River Damour at El Aliqa; this now meant that the southern suburbs of Beirut were within range of their 25-pdrs. The 2/16th West Australians spearheaded the attack. There would be heavy fighting throughout the day.

The French defences near Deir ez Zor were outflanked and one of the airfields near Aleppo was captured, including nine aircraft. It is believed that they were probably Bloch MB200s, as very little mention is made of these aircraft after 6 July.

Hurricanes belonging to 260/450 Squadron had flown up to Damascus late on 5 July and they launched a surprise attack at dawn on 6 July against Baalbeck. Finding very few targets, they moved on to Madjaloun, catching four Martin M167Fs in the process of taking off. All of the aircraft were shot up but not destroyed and this now meant that *Flotille* 4F was pretty much out of action, as they had no serviceable aircraft left. *Escadrille* 1AC, with six Dewoitine 520s, was already aloft, as their job was to have been to escort the Martins. They now engaged the Hurricanes. Although there was some damage to both the Hurricanes and the Dewoitines, neither side suffered any losses. More French naval fighters intercepted Flying Officer Waymark of C Flight, 208 Squadron. His Hurricane was damaged over Damour, but he managed to return home intact. The French began trying to evacuate aircraft from Syria on 6 July, with five Potez 63-11s of GAO583 heading for Athens.

The air war was still not over, but on the ground the Australians were closing in on Beirut and *Habforce* was now just thirty-five miles from Homs.

At around 0600 hours on 7 July five Dewoitine 520s of GCIII/6 lifted off to attack British columns to the north-west of Raqqa. In the engagement the aircraft flown by *Capitaine* Rivals-Mazères was badly damaged and he had to make a forced landing in the desert. Rivals-Mazères walked twenty miles to get back to his own lines.

Nearly seven hours later, six Dewoitine 520s of *Escadrille* 1AC, along with three more from GCIII/6 and three from GCII/3, covered four LeO451s of GBI/31, three from GBI/12 and seven from GBI/25 in an attack on Royal Navy vessels off Damour. The attack caused very little damage and was not intercepted by RAF aircraft. However, this was not the case when a number of Ju88s belonging to II/LG1, operating out of Crete, made an attack on the same Royal Naval vessels. This time they were pounced on by Hurricanes of 80 Squadron and at least two of the Ju88s were badly damaged.

The Morane 406 of *Adjutant Chef* Amarger of GCI/7 intercepted incoming Wellingtons of 70 Squadron, who had flown up from

Egypt to make a night-bombing attack that night. In a confusing fight in the pitch black one of the Wellingtons was badly damaged and it crash-landed when it returned to base.

On the ground, as well as in the air, the situation was beginning to look decidedly bleak for the Vichy French. High Commissioner Dentz had approached the US Consul General, Van Engert, to enquire what the British terms might be for a ceasefire. Somehow, the news leaked out and Australia's Minister for External Affairs, Sir Frederick Stewart, announced that the Vichy French had asked for an end to hostilities in Syria. The news story was soon being repeated by the BBC. General Lavarck was livid that the story had leaked out and said: 'Knowledge of the possibility of an armistice will make troops less inclined to do the things which so often mean the difference between success and failure. No man is likely to risk his life unnecessarily if he feels the campaign is virtually over.'

The campaign, in fact, was far from over and, although resistance and defences were beginning to crumble, the French were counter-attacking wherever possible.

Already, the Vichy Air Force was beginning to step up its withdrawal, however. After flying strafing missions around Raqqa and then escorting LeO451s against the Royal Navy, GCIII/6 was given orders at 2000 hours to withdraw to Athens. Pilots that still had an aircraft were to make their own way and the remaining pilots and ground crew would leave on an Air France D338. At the same time, GBI/12 and GBI/31 and their LeO451s were also told to head for Athens. This was, however, a confusing set of orders, as additional aircraft were actually arriving in Syria. Five Martin M167Fs belonging to GRI/22 arrived at Aleppo. A pair of Potez 63-11s also arrived but there would be no retreat for the remaining Morane 406s, as they could not carry sufficient fuel to fly to the comparative safety of Greece.

On 9 July Damour fell to the Australians, but the LeO451s of GBI/25 were still active, attacking targets around Raqqa. On the same day, Lieutenant de V. Clavel arrived at Aleppo at 1100 hours. He had brought with him three LeOH-257Bis biplane bombers, belonging to Aéronavale Escadrille 1E. The newly arrived aircraft's engines were still hot, having only been on the ground for around an hour when suddenly, at around midday, ten Hurricanes belonging to 260/450 Squadron came in to attack. One of the LeOs burst into flames and the other two were shot up. There was additional damage to a Martin 167F, a Farman 222.1, a 222.3 and the High Commissioner's own Potez 540TOE transport.

There were more Vichy aircraft departures on 10 July, with the Australians only five miles from Beirut and the road between Damascus and Beirut severed for good. Fourteen Dewoitine 520s of GCIII/6 left Mousilimiya at 0530 hours. Later the remaining eight LeO451s of GBI/31 also departed. Seven Martin M167Fs of GBI/39 headed home, as did seven LeO451s of GBI/12. The majority of them would make it back safely, although one of GBI/12's aircraft would have to force-land on the Turkish coast and the crew would be interned. One of the Martins belonging to GBI/39 would crash-land on Corfu on 14 July.

These were not the only departures of the day. *Escadrille* 1AC sent back three of their Dewoitine 520s, *Escadrille* 19S despatched three LeO130s and a single Martin 7B-1 had left Madjaloun bound for Athens at 1430 hours. It was not to make it, however, and some miles to the south of Cyprus one of the engines seized. It had been damaged in a strafing attack four days earlier. The pilot turned the aircraft around and made a landing at Beirut, where it was sub-sequently abandoned.

3 RAAF Squadron was up to the usual trick of strafing airfields. This time they hit Hama at 0815 hours, setting fire to a pair of LeO451s belonging to GBI/25. The LeO451s of this squadron, un-perturbed, launched attacks on drinking water tanks at T4 on two different occasions during the day.

There was an aerial engagement shortly after 1030 hours on 10 July when a number of French aircraft had taken off from Madjaloun to bomb British vehicles around Khalde. They were escorted by five Dewoitine 520s belonging to *Escadrille* 1AC. At the same time, twelve Blenheims of 45 Squadron were roaring in to make attacks on an ammunition dump to the south of Beirut, covered by seven Australian Tomahawks. They hit the target and there were huge explosions. The French naval Dewoitine 520s engaged the Blen-heims, shooting down three of them, damaging another one that subsequently crash-landed when it returned to base and shooting up six more. Now the Australian Tomahawks arrived on the scene.

Flying Officer Turnbull, Flying Officer J.F. Jackson, Pilot Officer Lane and Sergeant Hiller all claimed kills; in fact, five French fighters in total. In reality, two of the Dewoitines had been shot down.

Palmyra airfield, now in British hands, was home to B Flight Lysanders of 208 Squadron and Gladiators of X Flight. GCII/3 had launched a dozen Dewoitine 520s at 0500 hours on 11 July and they came in to strafe the airfield at daybreak. In the attack they damaged two Gladiators, set a Lysander on fire and damaged a second.

The end game as far as the air combat was concerned was close, but not before Palmyra airfield received massive reinforcement. Six Tomahawks flew in, followed by six Hurricanes of 80 Squadron, closely followed by another six from 260/450 Squadron. They were all to refuel and launch a major attack on the Aleppo airfields in the afternoon.

The Tomahawks and Hurricanes lifted off at 1200 hours, at about the same time as three LeO451s, escorted by nine of GCII/3's Dewoitine 520s, which launched their last sortie against the Damour and Khalde area. The Dewoitine flown by Lieutenant Lété experienced engine problems and lost contact with the rest of the aircraft. Suddenly, he saw three Tomahawks and attacked. He shot down Flying Officer F. Fisher's aircraft then Flying Officer R. Gibbes shot him down. The Frenchman crash landed near Hama. As for Fisher, he, too, survived, having hidden in an Arab village until the armistice came into force.

The Tomahawks and Hurricanes went on to attack Hama, where they caught a number of LeO451s belonging to GBI/25 on the ground. One of them burst into flames and then exploded, two more were smashed to pieces and five others suffered damage.

The final operation carried out by the RAF in the campaign took place when six Tomahawks attacked French positions in the Djebel Manzar area. One of the Tomahawks, flown by Flying Officer Knowles, was hit by anti-aircraft fire and crash-landed ten miles from Damascus.

By the evening of 11 July General Dentz had received the Allied terms of surrender and requested that hostilities cease at midnight. Hostilities finally ended at 0001 hours on 12 July 1941. But it was not quite as simple as that, as certain units were out of radio contact.

Consequently, eleven Morane 406s were prowling around on the morning of 12 July and a number of them, all belonging to GCI/7, strafed vehicles near Raqqa.

As many of the other remaining Vichy French aircraft as possible attempted to leave Syria. *Flotille* 4F's remaining four Martin M167s headed for Rhodes at 0800 hours. They were then followed by a quartet of Dewoitine 520s belonging to *Escadrille* 1AC and followed up by the Late 298s. A little later what remained of GBI/25's LeO451s made for Athens, along with the thirteen remaining Dewoitine 520s of GCII/3.

Casualties during the Syrian campaign are somewhat difficult to comprehend. According to French sources, 1,092 French officers and men had been killed in the campaign, although total Vichy casualties amounted to some 6,000, but this included men that had deserted to the Free French. The French that remained in Syria were given the choice by the British Government as to whether to join the Free French or to be repatriated. Of the 37,735, only 5,668 decided to take the Free French option. Some 37,000 military and civilian personnel would need to be shipped to mainland France.

A large number of British prisoners had been taken during hostilities and, in fact, the British casualties, including the Australians, amounted to some 3,300. In order to secure the British prisoners' return General Dentz and twenty-nine other French senior officers would remain in British hands. The Free French had lost around 1,300.

The Vichy French Air Force, by and large, had acquitted itself fairly well. At the beginning of hostilities they had had 234 aircraft, either in Syria or en route. An additional thirty-nine had been sent out, giving them a total of 273. They had lost forty-five of them on the ground, twenty in accidents, fifty-four abandoned owing to serious damage, sixteen to anti-aircraft fire and twenty-six in aerial combat. In addition to this, around thirty or so had been lost either flying to, or leaving Syria. Ignoring these thirty, the Vichy French had lost 169 aircraft. This is in comparison to a total of forty-one that had been lost by British units. Three of the British aircraft had been wrecked on the ground, four had been shot down by anti-aircraft guns and twenty-seven to air combat. Despite the fact that the French had done their utmost to get as many of the aircraft out of

Syria as possible before the armistice, they had left behind a large number of planes, including eleven Morane 406s.

Despite the fact that the French had lost Syria, they had not lost their will to resist. In fact, Laval, who had narrowly escaped assassination and been dismissed in February 1941, was quoted as saying:

> France does not want to be liberated. She wants to settle her fate herself in collaboration with Germany. Would the United States want to push France into a contrary peace, a peace of destruction and division, by urging her to spurn the extended hand of Hitler – a hand extended in a gesture quite unique in history?

Laval had come extremely close to death on 27 August 1941 at Versailles, when he was inspecting French volunteers prepared to fight on the eastern front against the Russians alongside the German army.

As Laval spent the remainder of the year convalescing, 1942 would begin to see a definite turning of the tide and sooner or later Pétain, Darlan and Laval would realize that they had backed the wrong horse.

Chapter Six

Operation *Ironclad*

The unexpected Japanese attack on Pearl Harbor in December 1941 had been the precursor to a series of unmitigated disasters for not just the United States, but also the British and their Commonwealth allies and other European states, including France. In short order, Burma, Singapore, the Philippines, the Dutch East Indies and Malaya had all fallen to the Japanese. India was under threat and in New Guinea, US troops and Australians were doing their best to stem the Japanese tide.

It had not just been the Americans that had lost vessels at Pearl Harbor; the British had lost HMS *Prince of Wales* and HMS *Repulse*. The Japanese had penetrated the Indian Ocean and were sinking merchant ships at will. They were also threatening Ceylon (Sri Lanka) by launching massive air attacks on the naval bases.

In March 1942, the British had not endeared themselves greatly to the French. On 3 March, 235 RAF bombers had levelled the Renault factory at Billancourt, near Paris. Around 400 civilians had been killed. Whilst the French were livid and Darlan had written to Admiral Leahy, the US Ambassador to Vichy, there was a good reason why the factory had been targeted. It was engaged in making trucks for the German army.

Darlan had written: 'We shall never forgive them. To murder, for political motives, women, children and old people is a method of Soviet inspiration.'

That was not all; in order to deny the German battleship *Tirpitz* a safe haven on the Atlantic coast, an operation had been launched against St Nazaire. The dry dock there had originally been built for the now capsized French liner, *Normandie*. Churchill had authorized the outrageously daring operation.

The former USS *Buchanan*, now renamed HMS *Campbeltown*, had been refitted with a 3-ton time bomb. Her heavy guns had been stripped out and her crew reduced. On board, however, were commando demolition parties and she was accompanied by a number of motor launches carrying more commandos. She had slipped into the Loire estuary and at 0125 hours on 28 March 1942 she was close to her target. She had fooled the Germans into believing that she was not as she seemed. But just a mile from the dockyard she ran up the white ensign, steamed through the torpedo net and, at a speed of 20 knots, rammed the dock gates. Commandos scrambled off the launches to assault German defensive positions, whilst the other commandos left satchel charges to wreck the machinery. Setting the time fuses, what remained of the force, now reduced to six boats and many wounded, beat a hasty retreat.

German engineers clambered aboard and at 1130 hours declared that she was safe. The fuses had supposed to have gone off at 0900 hours. As it was they chose to go off now, taking with them 250 Germans and French. The docks were irreparably damaged. It had been a bloody assault, with 169 commandos and sailors killed, and 214 captured. Twenty-seven of them managed to get home and another twenty-two, by circuitous routes, got to Gibraltar.

Shortly afterwards, by mid-April, Laval was back in power in France. One of the first discussions he had was whether to declare war on Britain, so certain was he that the Germans would eventually triumph.

France's fortunes and the strategic ambitions of the Japanese were about to coincide. Churchill and the British, as well as the Americans, were all-too certain that the Vichy French were happy to come to terms with the Japanese. There was precedent for it; back on 10 December 1941, Japanese torpedo bombers, based on Indochina airfields owned by Vichy France, had been responsible for the sinking of HMS *Prince of Wales* and HMS *Repulse*. Churchill, in particular, had been furious.

French fortunes in the Far East were in chaos. Thailand had been involved in a war with the French in order to reclaim territory that they believed to belong to them. The war had lasted between October 1940 and 9 May 1941. There had been a minor sea battle that had taken place on 17 January 1941, where one French light cruiser, four sloops and nine aircraft had beaten a Thai coastal defence ship, two torpedo boats and a handful of aircraft. The war actually came to an end at the instigation of the Japanese. The Vichy French regime had granted Japan access to Tonkin on 22 September 1940. But fighting had broken out and the Vichy French had lost the struggle, thus allowing the Japanese virtual control of Vichy French Indochina.

So there was precedent for the Vichy French coming to terms with the Japanese. Eyes began to fall on the isolated French possession of Madagascar. France's association with this country dated back to the seventeenth century, when the French East India Company had attempted to establish a colony on the island. It was during the reign of Queen Ranavalona I that Christians, amongst whom there were French citizens, were persecuted and had their property seized. This precipitated the Franco-Malagasy war, which was, in fact, a series of French military expeditions between 1883 and 1896. There were two phases of this war, but by the end of it Madagascar was annexed, ending the 103-year native monarchy, and the royal family was exiled to Algeria.

The Madagascar of 1940, post-armistice, was decidedly Vichy. It was, therefore, a considerable temptation to believe that the Vichy Government could offer the Japanese the opportunity to set up a base to service their submarines, which were wreaking such havoc in the Indian Ocean.

Madagascar is a large island, in fact bigger than France, and the fourth largest island in the world. It is 1,000 miles long and up to 400 miles wide. By 1942 the population was around 4,000,000, the vast majority of whom were native Malagasy, who could trace their ancestry back to Indonesia. There were around 25,000 French on the island, mainly colonial civil servants. In addition, there were Africans, Asians, Chinese and other Europeans.

The governor of the island, Jules Marcel de Coppet, had shown distinct Gaullist tendencies, although he was a socialist. He had been replaced by Léon Cayla who had been the governor from 1930 to 1939 and had retired due to health reasons. But now he was back. Madagascar was positioned close to South Africa, Kenya and Tanganyika, making it extremely exposed and isolated.

Initially, the British had kept an eye on Madagascar purely by inserting special operations executive (SOE) agents on the island. These kept in contact using secret radios. Strategically, Madagascar was in a very important position. Britain supplied Egypt by sending vessels around the Cape, through the Mozambique Channel, into the Red Sea and then up the Suez Canal. This was a much longer, but more preferable route than attempting the mad dash across the Mediterranean from Gibraltar. As far as the Royal Navy was concerned, they would sleep more peacefully at night if the main port of Diego Suarez was in British hands. It was unthinkable that the port be handed over to the Japanese; not only was it big enough for the entire Japanese fleet to sit in, but in 1935 France had put in oil bunkers, jetties and coastal batteries. If the French could be persuaded to allow the Japanese to use it there was a very good chance that the long supply route to Egypt would be severed.

As a consequence, on 23 December 1941, Major General Robert Sturges of the Royal Marines was appointed the commander of Force 121. At the heart of the force was the 29th Independent Brigade Group, commanded by Brigadier Francis Festing. The brigade consisted of the 1st Royal Scots Fusiliers, the 2nd Royal Welsh Fusiliers, the 2nd Lancashire's, the 2nd East Lancashire's, an independent artillery battery and four Bofors guns for anti-aircraft work. They were given the job of launching Operation *Ironclad* and to ensure that they had sufficient resources they were given No. 5 Commando and the Royal Armoured Corps' Special Service B Squadron. This consisted of six Valentine tanks and six Tetrarch reconnaissance tanks.

It had already been decided to seize Diego Suarez before the Japanese took it. On 12 March 1942 the British War Cabinet rubber-stamped Operation *Ironclad* and put Rear Admiral Neville Syfret as its combined commander. They would also earmark 12,000 men from the 5th Division, who were en route to India, to be made available for the Madagascar campaign.

According to South African military historian Colonel J.A. Clayton:

Before the invasion took place, Japanese ships were found to be using Madagascar. On 17 February 1942, three Japanese warships were reported by agents to be in Diego Suarez harbour. An immediate request was made by the British government to South Africa for a photo reconnaissance of the harbour. Two SAAF Glen Martin Maryland bomber aircraft, fitted with special long range tanks and cameras, under the command of Maj Bert Rademan, were immediately despatched to Lindi on the East African coast, this being the nearest place for a crossing to Diego Suarez. They flew the 700 miles (1,120 km) across the Indian Ocean, carried out the photo reconnaissance in unfavourable weather conditions, and returned to Lindi. On 12 March 1942, a further photo reconnaissance was carried out at the urgent request of the British government, this time by Maj Ken Jones and Capt M.J. Uys in two specially-equipped Maryland aircraft. Flying through severe tropical storms, they managed to photograph much of the area in spite of poor weather conditions. Six merchant ships, a cruiser and two submarines were seen in the harbour. The crews of the Marylands deserved the highest praise for sitting in the cramped cockpits for eight to nine hours, confronted by dreadful weather. The results of the reconnaissance flights were immediately transmitted to the British government and provided the planning staff with valuable information.

By 5 April all of the vessels involved in the operation had reached Freetown in Sierra Leone. Only a handful of the men actually knew their destination. Once they were back out to sea the men were briefed; they were to capture Diego Suarez harbour and D-Day was set for 0400 hours on 5 May.

The French had managed with a handful of Potez 25TOE army cooperation biplanes on Madagascar until the middle of 1941. In January 1941 the Vichy French had decided to create *Escadrille* 565, which was supposed to have received Morane 406 fighters. As it was, nothing had happened until the end of July 1941. Some thirteen pilots had already been sent to Arrachart airfield, some seven miles to the south of Diego Suarez. They were under the command of *Capitaine* Leonetti. When the men arrived without their aircraft they found that the airfield was in a dreadful mess. All they could do was to try to sort the airfield out and fly some training sorties in the Potez

25TOEs. On 23 July seven Potez 63-11s arrived on board SS *Bangkok*. They were sent to Ivato-Tananarive, which was in the centre of the island.

By October 1941 the first of the Morane 406s arrived and it was decided in February 1942 to put all of the Moranes and the Potez 63-11s under a unified command. Although figures are sketchy, it does appear that around twenty Moranes were sent to Madagascar. Ground troops on Madagascar amounted to something in the region of 8,000. The vast majority of them were native Malagasy, although there were some Senegalese and French troops. The garrison of Diego Suarez was around 3,000, supported by mule-drawn 75 mm guns, five coastal batteries, a handful of anti-tank guns and some anti-aircraft weapons.

The approach to Diego Suarez harbour was perilous; not only was it covered by the coastal battery, which was in telephone contact with an observation post, but also there were reefs, shoals and mines. There were also some two miles of pillboxes and trenches built around the dockyards. There was a pair of redoubts made of concrete, known as Forts Caimans and Bellevue.

In truth, however, these defences, known as the Joffre Line, were in a serious state of disrepair. Whole stretches of the trench system were covered in vegetation, but the French set about putting them back in order, as well as impressing civilians to build an anti-tank ditch.

The first part of the British force left Durban on 25 April 1942, consisting of the cruiser HMS *Devonshire*, and a pair of destroyers, along with some corvettes and minesweepers. On 28 April the assault ships, along with the cruiser HMS *Hermione*, the battleship HMS *Ramilles* and the aircraft carrier HMS *Illustrious* and six destroyers, departed.

Colonel J.A. Clayton detailed the air assets available to the invasion force and the orders given to the SAAF units:

Royal Navy Fleet Air Arm (Aircraft Carriers)
795 Squadron Fairey Fulmar aircraft.
796 Squadron Albacore aircraft.
One Squadron Swordfish Torpedo Bombers.
Two Squadrons Martlet Fighters.

RAF

443 Army Co-op. Flight of six Lysander aircraft brought in by ship.

SA Air Force

Three Maritime Reconnaissance Flights, later combined to form 16 Squadron: No. 32 Flight – five Glenn Martin Maryland Bombers (Major D. Meaker, Officer Commanding); No. 36 Flight – six Bristol Beaufort Bombers (Major J. Clayton, Officer Commanding); and No. 37 Flight – one Maryland and five Beauforts (Major K. Jones, Officer Commanding).

Seven flights numbered 31 to 37, using Ansons, Marylands, Beauforts and Ju86s, were detailed to patrol the seas around South Africa. Three of the flights were withdrawn (32, 36 and 37). These would be used as the SAA component for the invasion force and placed under the command of Colonel S.A. Melville.

The aircraft were mustered at Swartkops air station at Pretoria on April 28 1942. With such a mix of different aircraft there were bound to be problems. The Bristol Beaufort, originally designed as a torpedo bomber, had a pair of what proved to be very unreliable Bristol Taurus engines. It was a heavy aircraft, but it was impossible to fly due to its weight with just one engine. It was, however, strong and could be crash landed without wheels on fairly rough ground without imperilling the crew. It had excellent visibility and space. The Glenn Martin Maryland was cramped by comparison; however it had far more reliable Pratt and Whitney engines.

The engineers discovered that there were considerable problems with the Taurus engine. There was a metal sleeve inside each cylinder that moved up and down and rotated. This uncovered the ports in the cylinder wall. The piston worked up and down within the sleeve and this arrangement was prone to seizing, which would cause the engines to stop. Each of the engines had eighteen of these cylinders, so collectively there were thirty-six, hence there was a lot that could go wrong.

Some thirty-five Beauforts were supposed to replace the Ansons; eighteen of them arrived and were put together at

Cape Town but four were lost. Lieutenant Binkie Stewart's aircraft came down over the sea and Lieutenant McPherson crash landed in a pine forest near Cape Town.

The South African aircraft were finally ready to leave Swartkops on May 6 1942. They headed for Lusaka and from there they made for Kasama, losing another Beaufort due to engine problems. Lieutenant McPherson, now in another Beaufort, came down near the Bangwelu swamp and was lucky to escape for a second time. A ground party, commanded by Lieutenant Jock Bell, along with police officers, retrieved him and his crew.

The ultimate destination of the force was Lindi, on the coast. In command would be Lieutenant Colonel Jimmy Durrant, who had been ordered to set up a forward air base. Now the South Africans would have to wait until the initial landings by the British at Diego Suarez had been successful and had managed to secure an airfield.

There would be a lot of work to be done before Clayton and the others received their signal.

The fleet passed to the west of Madagascar and on 3 May joined up with HMS *Indomitable*, along with two escorting destroyers. It was hoped that the two air groups would be sufficient to eliminate the Vichy French Air Force and to supply sufficient support for the ground troops. Meanwhile, the Royal Navy Eastern Fleet, including the aircraft carrier, HMS *Formidable*, was patrolling the Indian Ocean just in case the Japanese chose to intervene. By midday on 4 May, the spearhead of the vessels involved in the operation rounded Cap d'Amer, on the northern tip of Madagascar. It was so far so good; the French had no idea that the invasion force had arrived.

The first wave of assault craft hit the beaches at around dawn on 5 May. The lead elements consisted of 5 Commando and the East Lancashire's. Surprise was nearly ruined when one of the minesweepers exploded two mines. Incredibly, they caught the French, literally, asleep. The gunners that were supposed to be manning the coastal defences were rounded up. Only one of the French officers resisted, but he was shot through the forehead. Thus, the battery at Courrier was taken with, literally, one shot.

Just before dawn HMS *Illustrious* launched three strikes, each consisting of six Swordfish, to attack shipping in Diego Suarez bay.

Albacores, meanwhile, headed to bomb Arrachart airfield. The beaches and the bombing attacks were covered by fighters. The Swordfish sank the armed merchant cruiser *Bougainville* and then the submarine *Bévéziers*. One of the aircraft, flown by Lieutenant Robert Everett, RN, was shot down by anti-aircraft fire. He and his crew were taken prisoner. Everett had been dropping leaflets in French in order to encourage the Vichy troops to surrender and to justify Britain's actions against Madagascar.

As the Albacores and Martlets hit Arrachart airfield they had caught the majority of the French aircraft napping. Five of the Morane 406s were destroyed and another two damaged, as was a pair of the Potez 63-11s. The French detachment commander, Lieutenant Rossigneux, was killed in the attack. At a stroke, the Vichy air strength on the island had been reduced by 25 per cent. As soon as the British landings became known, a number of Potez 63-11s and Morane 406s were hastily flown up to Anivorano, some fifty miles to the south of Diego Suarez.

Meanwhile, on the ground advanced units of the Royal Welsh Fusiliers had come across a French officer in a car. He was deliberately not blindfolded, so that he could see the full strength of the invasion force. Subsequently, the same officer would be sent back to his own headquarters to deliver a message from the British, calling on the French to surrender. However, the Frenchman had seen everything he needed; it was clear exactly where the British were heading and this gave the Vichy commander on the island, Annet, enough time to get his mobile reserves and anti-tank guns into the Joffre Line. By 1115 hours French troops were firing back, holding a ridge line. But this was forced by the British and by 1500 hours the French had fallen back to the Joffre Line.

A vessel that had been missed by the British in Diego Suarez bay earlier, the sloop *D'Entrecasteaux*, was finished off by four Swordfish. Navy Martlets and Fulmars were flown on reconnaissance sorties. The only sign of the French Air Force had taken place at around 1700 hours, when a pair of Morane 406s had strafed the beaches of Courrier Bay. The aircraft flown by Sergeant Ehret never returned and his fate is unclear. The French lost another aircraft that day, again under strange circumstances. It was a Potez 63-11 flown by Lieutenant Schlienger and it is possible that it was shot down by British ground fire.

The French did launch an attack at around 0600 hours on 6 May 1942, when three Potez 63-11s attempted to attack the beach landing points. They were intercepted by Martlets of 881 Squadron. In the ensuing fight Lieutenant Bird and Sub-Lieutenant J. Waller shot one of them down and a second was claimed by Lieutenant C.C. Tomkinson. Albacores were used to bomb French defences, whilst Sub-Lieutenant F.H. Alexander, in his Swordfish, managed to sink the French submarine *Le Heros*, with depth charges. By the early hours of 7 May the residual French resistance before the Joffre Line had been worn down.

The plan was now to strike east, from Ambararata towards Antsirane. In fact, the British force had achieved an eighteen-mile advance in some twenty-four hours. It was decided to launch a diversionary attack by the fifty or so Marines, commanded by Captain Martin Price, on board HMS *Ramillies*. HMS *Anthony* circled around the northern tip of Madagascar and delivered the men for their diversionary attack.

HMS *Anthony* approached at high speed, coming under fire from the shore batteries. The destroyer landed fifty Royal Marines, under the command of Captain Martin Price, RM, at around 2000 on May 6 1942. The men scrambled onto the quay at Antsirane and stormed the French army barracks. They also took the arsenal and scooped 500 prisoners. HMS *Anthony* then left the harbour and crashed through the boom at the harbour entrance. At that point a French searchlight found her, but a salvo from HMS *Devonshire* wrecked the searchlight and enabled the vessel to return to the anchorage. It took twenty-four rounds of 15-inch shells from HMS *Ramillies* to persuade the gun batteries in the forts on the Orangia Peninsular to surrender on the afternoon of May 6. By this time British and allied forces had managed to secure their first objectives.

At the same time, a determined attack was made on the Joffre Line. The two leading battalions, the 6th Seaforth Highlanders and the 2nd Northamptons, took up start positions barely 1,200 yards from French trenches. Behind them were the Royal Scots Fusiliers and the 2nd Royal Welsh Fusiliers. The attack was timed to coincide with the landing of the Commandos. HMS *Anthony* passed the entrance batteries unharmed and came along the quayside at 2200 hours. She dropped off the Marines and then went back out to sea. It was half an hour before the British infantry had got on their feet and had begun to storm the main French defence lines. With a combination of grenades and bayonet attacks all of the strong points were taken and before dawn on 7 May 1942 British troops were well established in Antsirane.

The battle for Madagascar was by no means over. Overhead, Martlets of 888 Squadron encountered, for the first and only time, French fighters. Three Morane 406s flown by *Capitaine* Leonetti, *Capitaine* Bernache-Assollant and Lieutenant Laurent were spotted on a reconnaissance mission. One of the Martlets was shot down by Leonetti, whilst Sub-Lieutenant J.A. Lyon claimed that he had shot down one of the French fighters, but he was probably mistaken. A second group of Martlets dived down to assist. Lieutenant Tomkinson was to claim one Morane 406 and Sub-Lieutenant (A) Waller claimed a second. The pair of them then attacked a third French fighter. It is clear that all three French aircraft were lost, with one of the pilots killed, one wounded and another injured as he hit the ground having baled out. The operation, so far, had claimed twelve Morane 406s, and perhaps five Potez 63-11s, out of a comparatively small French force.

By 1040 hours on 7 May, British warships opened up a barrage on Diego Suarez. British minesweepers began clearing the channel into the harbour and by 1700 hours the Royal Navy was also in the harbour. The French were already negotiating surrender terms.

But this was only a part of Madagascar. In fact, the capture of the capital had changed very little. Undoubtedly, the momentum was with the British, but the French would drag their feet, hoping that the rainy season would begin and buy them time. So far, the Fleet Air Arm had completed over 300 sorties. There was now an opportunity to reorganize the air components in Madagascar. Finally, 20 SAAF Squadron could come in to Madagascar as had been planned.

The signal that Clayton and the others had been waiting for finally arrived on May 13 1942. Some thirty-four aircraft, including six Marylands, eleven Beauforts, twelve Lockheed Lodestars and six Ju52s, made for Diego Suarez. The Ju52s and Lodestars carried the spares and the maintenance personnel. They would not be staying and would return with Durrant to South Africa. It took the aircraft four hours to cover the 740 miles across the Indian Ocean. The small air fleet was fortunate not to lose a single aircraft and they landed at Arrachart airfield, just outside of Diego Suarez and some five miles to the south of Antsirane. Colonel Melville joined the men, but the airfield was still not secure and came under occasional sniper fire for several days.

It was going to be a frustrating time, as it was not until 27 May 1942 that Governor General Annet finally sent an emissary, in the shape of Lionel Barnett, who was an Englishman, to negotiate with the British at Diego Suarez. Barnett was probably connected to the Special Operations Executive and knew perfectly well that Annet was hoping that he could string the British along until November. This was when the seasonal rains would make it impossible to launch any further operations.

It was an uneasy period and, in any case, the bulk of the British forces was actually needed elsewhere. So time was very much of the essence. Nonetheless, British and Commonwealth troops began to settle down to their occupation duties, mindful of the fact that they might have to recommence hostilities at any time, or be posted to another theatre.

The SAAF men were now firmly established at Arrachart airfield. They used a pair of damaged hangars for essential aircraft maintenance work and inside they had found damaged or burned out French aircraft, which had to be removed first. The runway had an incline and the direction of the wind always meant that takeoffs were uphill, towards mountains. There was a valley at the end of the runway, so the aircraft could gain enough speed before having to turn sharply away from the mountains. Air operations were varied; there were anti-submarine and anti-shipping patrols along the east and west coasts of Madagascar, the aircraft made attacks on enemy strongholds and airfields to the south and carried out reconnaissance flights. Of great importance was mapping the road network on the island. This also involved photographic sorties so that the inaccurate maps that the invasion force was working from could be corrected. This was essential before any offensive to the south could be made.

The SAAF flew its first operational sorties on May 15. The flying conditions were extremely challenging, with heavy tropical rain storms. The aircraft were flying over virtually unknown mountains and jungle and they also had to fly over the sea; all of this was from bases that were barely adequate for the aircraft. The SAAF kept the three flights largely separate, each with its own officers' mess. The men distinguished themselves by wearing different coloured berets; red, green and yellow.

The SAAF had managed to acquire a Citroen car and seven motorcycles, the latter being liberated from the British. The South Africans repainted the motorcycles and the car, but this did not fool British officers that came to see if they knew anything about the missing machines.

An anti-submarine flight, bound for Majunga 300 miles away, is thought to have been their first sortie, which was launched on May 15. There were submarines visible in the port, but the pair of Marylands destroyed three Potez bombers that were sitting on the airfield.

Madagascar was a huge island, but it only had three major high-ways running out of the capital, Tananarive. One led to Majunga, another led to Tamatave and the third to Fianarantsoa. The island had also just short of 550 miles of railway track. Diego Suarez, being in the north and unconnected by road, still meant nothing if the Japanese were granted permission to set up bases on the island or chose to seize the bulk of the island for themselves. There were already rumours that the Japanese were using Majunga as a re-fuelling depot for their submarines.

Many of the British troops had already left, or were about to leave Madagascar, with many bound for India. The Royal Navy could only afford to deploy a pair of Corvettes, HMS *Thyme* and HMS *Genista*, on anti-submarine duties in the immediate vicinity. HMS *Ramillies* was still at Madagascar and the worst fears about Japanese submarines were soon to be realized.

The Japanese had developed two-man midget submarines, known as Ko-Hyoteki. They were capable of going down to around 100 feet and carried a pair of torpedoes. The submarines were around 78 feet long, but only 10 feet high and 6 feet across. The Japanese had already deployed them against Pearl Harbor and three of these submarines had attempted to slip into Sydney harbour on 29 May 1942. It had not been a terribly successful operation. All the major targets, including the American cruiser USS *Chicago*, were missed. They had managed to sink a floating barracks with the result of twenty-one Australian sailors being killed.

On the same night, at around 2230 hours, a small seaplane landed in the water close to HMS *Ramillies*. It was spotted and the engine burst into life. The seaplane flew off before anyone could fire at it. It was a bold move by someone and it was not clear whether the aircraft had been Vichy, German or Japanese.

In fact, it was a Japanese seaplane that was used as a scout by large Japanese submarines. HMS *Ramillies* was moved to a new anchorage and the newly arrived South African aircraft were sent off to see if they could discover anything out in the Indian Ocean. It was like looking for a needle in a haystack and the job of the two Corvettes on anti-submarine duty was no easier. They had to guard a mile-long stretch of water against a vessel that was only 6 feet wide.

This was before a net had been rigged across the entrance to the harbour and, taking full advantage of it, Lieutenant Akeida Saburo and Petty Officer Takemoto Masami of the Imperial Japanese Navy slipped into the anchorage. The mother ship, the *I-20*, had positioned itself about nine miles to the east of the harbour entrance. There were to have been two midget submarines involved in the attack, but one of them had obviously floundered and a body was later discovered.

It was around 2025 hours on the night of 30 May when the whole of Diego Suarez and Antsirane were shaken by an enormous explosion. As people looked out to discover the source of the noise, they could see that the battleship HMS *Ramillies* was listing. There was chaos and no one knew quite what to do. The midget submarine had fired its first torpedo, which had blown a 20-foot hole in the port bow of HMS *Ramillies*. Shortly afterwards, the midget submarine had actually partially surfaced and it had been spotted by crewmen on board the tanker *British Loyalty*. The crew had been able to get in a few shots at it with their anti-aircraft gun.

Meanwhile, on board the battleship the internal lights had failed and the magazine compartments were flooding. HMS *Ramillies'* picket boat, armed with depth charges, began hunting the anchor-age. She was soon joined by the pair of Corvettes, who used their Asdic to help them.

At 2102 hours the midget submarine came up to periscope depth and fired a second torpedo, but, instead, it hit the *British Loyalty*, which had deliberately made itself a target to protect the battleship. Five of the Indian crewmen were killed and as the crew abandoned ship the tanker sank into 70 feet of water. At this point the Japanese midget submarine, its main armament expended, slipped back out to sea.

At this point the British had no idea who had been responsible for the attacks. As a precautionary measure HMS *Ramillies* was moved into shallower water and men worked around the clock to make her seaworthy. Portable pumps were flown in from Durban and three trawlers equipped with Asdic were sent to improve the defences of the harbour. Other vessels were brought in from the Maldives and the South Atlantic to hunt for the raider.

On 2 June British troops patrolling the coastal area north of Diego Suarez were approached by a local. He told them that two Chinese men had asked him for food and water. He went on to explain that they had pistols and one of them was carrying a sword. They were insistent that they were friends of the French and that they were enemies of the British.

What had happened was that the midget submarine had made for the rendezvous point with the mother ship, but its batteries had run down. The men were cornered towards the end of the morning of 2 June. The Japanese had walked nearly fifty miles to the pickup point where they were to have met the mother ship. The men of 5 Commando called on the Japanese to surrender. The British soldiers heard two shots; the Japanese had committed suicide rather than fall into enemy hands.

The South African Government, under General Jan Smuts, was particularly livid and perturbed by the attack on the harbour. He was adamant that the attack must have been made by either a Vichy or Japanese submarine, acting on Vichy intelligence. He urged that the Vichy presence on Madagascar be eliminated at the earliest possible opportunity and warned against appeasement, as it had proven to be a dangerous strategy. He urged Churchill to ensure the redoubling of the efforts to evict the Vichy from Madagascar.

In fact, Japanese submarines were operational along the whole of the Mozambique Channel and for the time being there was very little the British could do about it.

Commodore Ishizaki, the Japanese fleet commander, had five vessels; three of them carried the midget submarines and Glenn Martin scout aircraft. It had actually been one of these that had cheekily landed beside HMS *Ramillies*. The other two vessels were support ships, *Aikou Maru* and the *Hokoku Maru*. They were operational in the Mozambique Channel between 5 June and 10 July 1942. In the space of that short period of time they sank twenty-three merchant vessels. The *I-10* had sunk eight and the *I-20* seven of these. They had even used the supply ships to help sink one of the merchant ships and capture two more.

It was gradually dawning on the British and their Allies that something had to be done, but, following the disastrous battle of Midway fought between 4 and 7 June 1942, it was the Japanese that made the decision. They had lost four of their aircraft carriers and the Imperial Japanese Navy would never really recover from this defeat. As a result, Ishizaki was told to return to closer waters and thus the Japanese threat around Madagascar disappeared.

The British had already decided to re-launch the Madagascar campaign and to divert assets in order to achieve this. De Gaulle had even proposed to land Free French on the island and Annet had contacted the Vichy Government to ask for more assistance, particularly in the shape of aircraft. But the nearest Vichy base was French Somaliland and the best that the limited number of French aircraft there could achieve was nuisance raids against the British. This would only enrage Britain further and bring about the immediate occupation of French Somaliland. As a consequence, Annet quickly realized that they would be on their own; there would be no reinforcement.

In the period June to August 1942, 20 SAAF Squadron carried out comprehensive photographic reconnaissance missions to build up a picture of the interior of Madagascar, in preparation for a new offensive. On one occasion, after one of the Marylands was shot down by Vichy French anti-aircraft fire, French troops rushed to capture the crew. As they arrived on the scene they were brought under fire from the Vickers machine gun in the dorsal turret of the aircraft. The South African crew captured the Vichy patrol, marched their prisoners to the coast and rendezvoused with a British destroyer.

By August it was clear that the probable French air strength on Madagascar was down to four Morane 406s and three Potez 63-11s.

Before the new offensive on Madagascar got underway, there was another clash between Britain and France, in the shape of Operation *Jubilee*. Significantly, a substantial part of the invasion force, which was predominantly Canadian, comprised French-speaking volunteers from Quebec. It was a disastrous and somewhat ill-conceived gesture to show that Britain still had a sting in its tail. Over half of the 6,000 men that were involved in the operation failed to return home. Significantly, Pétain had congratulated the Germans for 'cleansing French soil of the invader'.

Back on Madagascar, approaches had been made to the British stating that the bulk of the French on the island actually wanted to come to terms with the British, but that to simply surrender was out of the question. They had to succumb to an insurmountable show of force.

Plans to complete the conquest of Madagascar were already well advanced. But resources were still thinly stretched. The new invasion convoy and landings would only be covered by a single aircraft carrier, HMS *Illustrious*. HMS *Indomitable* had already left to assist Malta. This meant that the Royal Naval aircraft available for new operations amounted to 881 Squadron's twelve Martlets, 806 Squadron's six Fulmars and eighteen Swordfish belonging to 810 Squadron and 829 Squadron.

The plan was that Majunga (now Mahajanga) would be seized and the 22nd East African Brigade, with South African armoured cars, would push down the 270-mile road to Tananarive. There would also be two diversions; Commandos would land at Morondava, some 600 miles further south than Majunga. Once the landings at Majunga were established the British 29th Brigade would re-embark from Majunga and be taken all the way around the island, to land at Tamatave. This would mean that the capital would be threatened from both the west and the east.

The operation got underway just before daylight on 10 September 1942. The Vichy, having surrendered over 3,000 troops at Diego Suarez, was down to around 4,800 supported by sixteen artillery pieces and, by this stage, probably five aircraft. The assault on Majunga, known as Operation *Stream*, was spearheaded by the Royal Welsh Fusiliers and the East Lancashire Regiment. They landed ten miles to the north of the town. The South Lancashire's and 5 Commando secured Majunga harbour. At dawn, Swordfish buzzed ominously over the port, although they made no attacks and there was no sign of French aircraft.

As soon as the port was in British hands the East African Rifles and the Marmon-Herrington Mark III armoured cars of the South Africans sped down the road. Although the distance to the capital was 270 miles, this was as the crow flies and the road route was more like 400 miles. It was important that they captured important bridges along the route. By 1600 hours on 10 September they had captured the first one, 99 miles inland. By dawn on 11 September they were approaching the second one, at a distance of 131 miles.

The French had tried to destroy the bridge, but all they had achieved was that the central span was sagging into the river and, at worse, part of the road was under 3 feet of water. As soon as they realized their mistake, at 0730 hours, *Capitaine* Baché, in a Potez 63-11, was sent to drop bombs to finish off the bridge. The attack was a failure.

The airfield at Majunga was now in British hands and elements of the air cover, including Lysanders, were brought down to begin operations. In the early hours of 12 September 1942 a pair of Marylands engaged Vichy French motor transport between the broken bridge at Betsiboka and Tananarive. One Maryland was hit by anti-aircraft fire, which killed the observer and knocked out one of the engines.

The French beyond the broken bridge set up a series of road-blocks. But it was not until 16 September that the advancing forces came up against serious opposition. They were trying to take a bridge over the Mamokomita River at Andriba when they ran into a company of Senegalese. The leading East African company, supported by armoured cars, 25-pdrs and mortars, took the position.

On 17 September Annet requested an armistice and a Maryland was sent to Ivato to pick up French negotiators. After discussions the French rejected the terms and they were flown back to Ivato on 18 September. Meanwhile, Tamatave surrendered after a three-minute bombardment. The 29th Brigade clambered ashore and now the race to capture Tananarive was on. For the East Africans and the South Africans progress was now relatively slow because the French had destroyed bridges and culverts, which meant that a great deal of engineering work had to be carried out.

At Tamatave a number of the South Lancashire's had taken the opportunity to clamber on board a train that had just entered the station. They steamed fifty miles down the coast and captured Brickaville, which was on the coast road to Tananarive before it turned inland.

As the two competing columns of British and Commonwealth troops converged on the capital, Vichy French resistance began to stiffen. This meant that the air assets would once more be required. The Vichy French aircraft were all now based at Fianarantsoa, way to the south of the capital. Estimates vary, but the *Groupe Aerien Mixte* probably now amounted to a pair of Morane 406s, one Potez 63-11, perhaps two Potez 25TOEs, a Potez 29 and a Phrygane.

The latter aircraft was a French light aircraft, which was a high-wing monoplane with a fixed undercarriage. The aircraft had first flown in October 1933 and had been built by Salmson, a French engineering company. Only twenty-five aircraft had been sold before the outbreak of the Second World War.

By 21 September the East Africans had closed to a strongly held Vichy position at Mahitsy. The position was held in depth on high ground. During the night of 21 September the positions were out-flanked, but two days of fighting lay ahead before the French finally abandoned the positions. They were now only thirty miles from the capital, but the French had dug in around another strongpoint, at Ahidatrino. The French would not put up a fight because as a column of 22nd Brigade approached them on 23 September the bulk of the Vichy troops fled and a handful held on for half an hour before they, too, fell back. This meant that at 1700 hours on 23 September the East Africans and the South African armoured cars entered the capital. Meanwhile, on the other side of the island, covered by 1433 Flight's Lysanders, the 29th Brigade advanced from Brickaville. They, too, arrived in the capital in time for a victory parade.

There was good news and bad news. The good news was that the French had left behind aerial photographs of all of their airfields on Madagascar. The bad news began with the French refusal to surrender. This was quickly followed by the realization that the bulk of the Vichy French troops still willing to fight had fled south towards Fianarantsoa. As Allied troops moved south to pursue them they discovered roadblocks. Across one short stretch of road there were twenty-nine stone walls, up to 18 feet across. On another half-mile stretch 800 trees had been chopped down.

Fianarantsoa was the only major centre of population left on Madagascar that was still in French hands, but it also was the home of what remained of the Vichy French Air Force.

On 25 September two South African Marylands dropped bombs on a Vichy-held fort just after dawn. They dropped sixteen 250 lb bombs on the Tananarive to Antisirabe road. There was a British loss during the day when a Fleet Air Arm Fulmar belonging to 795 Squadron went missing.

A single Morane 406, flown by Lieutenant Toulouse, was active between 28 and 30 September 1942. On the first two days he flew reconnaissance missions to the north of Antisirabe and on the final day he strafed vehicles leading the British advance.

A single Maryland was flown into Ivato to refuel and then sent on a reconnaissance mission to inspect Vichy landing grounds to the south of the capital. The results were negative.

The ground war continued with troops from Tanganyika entering Antisirabe on 2 October. South African troops had also landed at Tulear in the south-west of Madagascar. They were moving up towards the capital via Sakaraha. Another force had landed at Fort Dauphin in the far south-east of the island. The landings had not gone unobserved, however. *Capitaine* Baché, flying a Potez 25TOE, and a Morane 406 flown by *Sergeant Chef* du Coutrin, had buzzed the positions. Further reconnaissance was made by the Vichy on 3 October.

A number of aircraft were moved to Antisirabe and Ivato during the day of 3 October, in preparation for the last attacks. The Vichy

Farman 223-3 belonging to GT I/15, these were used to fly in ammunition to the beleagured ...hy garrison at Palmyra in late June 1941.

...ing Officer Turnbull of 3 SAAF Squadron on the left with Flying Officer Saunders. Turnbull was ... most successful allied pilot of the Syrian campaign.

Australians and RAF posed beside an abandoned Morane 406 left at Nerab airfield by GC I/7 due the fact it lacked sufficient range to reach Athens and escape Syria.

Australians with a 2-pounder anti-tank gun beside the remains of two Dewoitines that exploded o Nerab airfield.

utenant Tremolet beside his Curtiss Hawk aircraft of GC II/5 which was shot down over the lines 6 November 1939. In the dog fight, eight Me109s were shot down for this single Hawk.

rane 406s of GC III/1 in June 1940. These aircraft belong to the Escadrille 2e.

loch MB174 in North Africa shortly after the armistice in June 1940.

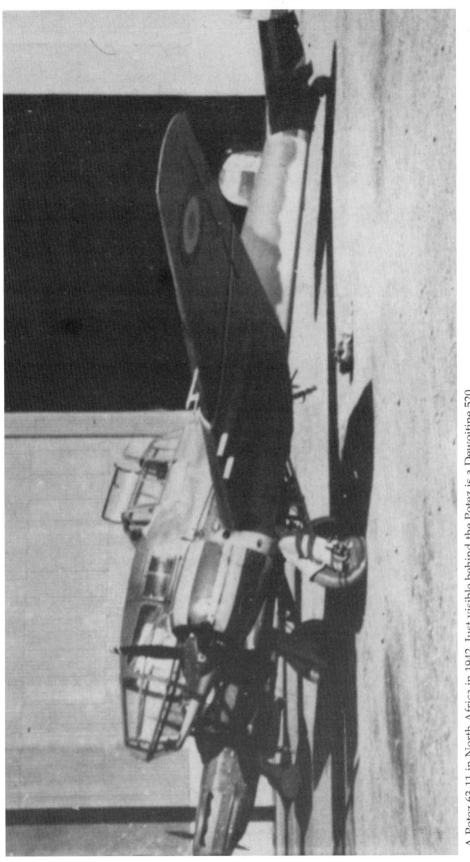

A Potez 63-11 in North Africa in 1942. Just visible behind the Potez is a Dewoitine 520.

A Dewoitine 520 of GC II/3 in Algeria in 1942.

General Giraud who had commanded the French 7th Army in France in 1940. He had been taken prisoner by the Germans but had escaped and was in hiding in Lyon. Escaping France, he met with Allied representatives who had great plans for him in North Africa.

US troops escorting a mixed bag of Vichy prisoners near Oran shortly after the Operation Torch landings.

senhower and Clarke flank Darlan during the crucial negotiations for the surrender of Vichy
orth Africa.

eneral Juin (right) and Generla Nogués (left) , both men supported Darlan's proposals to fall in
e with the Allies in North Africa.

Petain portrait in more happy times for the old soldier.

ajor General George S. Patton, Jr., Commander of US Forces in French Morocco compares notes at
mp Anfa, near Casablanca, with Vice Admiral Lord Louis Mountbatten of Great Britain, Chief of
mbined Operations. Photo was taken on the field the day President Roosevelt reviewed American
ops at the camp in January 1943.

The Casablanca conference.

ree members of the Free
ench foreign legion who
stinguished themselves in the
ttle at Bir Hacheim in the
estern desert. They are from
negal, Equatorial Africa, and
adagascar, respectively. Men
om the same regions of the
ench Empire were at the very
me time fighting for the Vichy.

Brazzaville 1942, French
Equatorial Africa. A tirailleur
(infantryman) who has been
warded the Cross of Liberation
by General Charles de Gaulle.

Free French anti-aircraft gunner in action in the Western desert in 1942.

Free French anti-aircra[ft] gunner in action on a merchant marine vess[el] in 1942.

ese French airplane engines were undamaged during Operation Torch and are in good working der. They will now be used against the Axis by the French air force in North Africa.

French Equatorial Africa cut off by the Royal Navy blockade from mainland France. African men and woman arriving at the monthly wild rubber village market, carrying rubber and supplies, Lebango, Moyen Congo, the photograph was taken in 1943.

Once Darlan had agreed to support the end of Vichy reistance in Algeria, the race was on to complete the occupation of the country before German and Italian intervention.

American and British military leaders at the Casablanca conference, Casablanca, Morocco in January 1943. Portrait includes Winston Churchill (seated third from left), Franklin D. Roosevelt (4th from left), and General Sir Alan Brooke (5th from left).

Air Force got in the first blow when *Sergeant Chef* Largeau in a Morane 406 strafed Bren gun carriers near Antinchi on 6 October. The British now responded by making offensive sweeps across all the known airfields on 7 October. A pair of Fulmars spotted a Potez 63-11 airborne, but the French pilot evaded them.

By now, the French aircraft had been pulled back to their new operational base at Ihosy. Aerial reconnaissance by a pair of Marylands, who also dropped bombs on the hangar there, confirmed that this was the main French aircraft concentration.

On 8 October three Beauforts came in to bomb Ihosy airfield. The French had been canny, however, and had positioned their aircraft in the bushes up to a mile away from the airfield itself. The Beaufort crews confirmed that they had seen three Potez 25TOEs, a Morane 406 and a Potez 63-11. The Beauforts strafed the targets, reporting that the Morane had been partially set on fire. They then radioed the positions to the incoming South African Marylands. The photographic evidence confirmed the situation; a Potez 25TOE had been set on fire and the Morane had certainly been hit. But the French had acted swiftly after the Beaufort attack and had moved the aircraft around to try and hide them even further. Another bombing attack wrecked one of the Potez 25TOEs. More attacks came in, which ultimately saw a Potez 29 and a Potez 63-11 also destroyed. Incredibly, the Morane was still intact and *Sergeant Chef* Largeau flew a reconnaissance mission on 12 October.

On the same day four Beauforts bombed the airfield again and three days later Marylands attacked Vichy positions to the south of Ambositra. The Vichy positions here were bombarded and the enemy troops finally surrendered as Commonwealth troops closed in.

The artillery barrage had broken up the positions and the Vichy forces had been attacked in the rear by the King's African Rifles. The commander of the French troops, Colonel Metras, and his headquarters also fell into British hands. By this stage the Vichy forces were down to around six depleted companies. They fell back towards Fianarantsoa.

At dawn on 20 October the Vichy forces suffered a frontal attack by Tanganyika infantry. At the same time South African armoured cars and Kenyan infantry worked around their flanks and captured 200 prisoners.

Incredibly, the Morane 406 was still operational and it had even launched strafing attacks on South African troops. However, by 21 October it was just the Salmson Phrygane that was left serviceable and it made its final sortie on 22 October, piloted by *Capitaine* Baché. The airfield at Ihosy was still being bombed as a precautionary measure, as were the final French ground force positions to the north of Alakamisy.

The armistice was finally signed in the early hours of 6 November 1942 and the former Vichy governor was flown to Tamatave. The French had finally surrendered some forty-two days after the capture of the capital. The ceasefire came into force at one minute past midnight on 6 November.

However, this would not be the last time that the Vichy Air Force would be in action against their former allies. On Sunday 8 November 1942 Operation *Torch* was launched, as the Anglo-American forces landed in French Algeria and Morocco.

Chapter Seven

Operation *Torch*

Under the terms of the armistice in 1940 the then Commander-in-Chief of French North African troops, General Nogués, had wanted to continue the fight. But this would have made the armistice negotiations impossible. In any case, North Africa lacked the manufacturing base to produce tanks and aircraft. It was the French position that if French North Africa remained in French hands and was not occupied by the Germans, then it would ultimately give them a stronger hand in negotiations with the Germans. The French army in North Africa began to demobilize to an extent, reducing to an agreed level of some 100,000 troops.

The attack on the French fleet at Oran by the British had created a very strong anti-British feeling, which was followed by the Vichy forces' refusal to back down at Dakar and, subsequently, their dogged resistance in Syria and in Madagascar. The new Commander-in-Chief of North Africa by the time that Operation *Torch* began to be mooted was General Weygand. He made sure that as much French equipment was hidden in Algiers, Tunis, Rabat and other places, so that it was not spotted by either the German or Italian armistice commissions.

North Africa remained solidly behind Vichy. It was divorced geographically from both the unoccupied and occupied parts of France. In fact, Weygand was very anti-German and patriotic and he struggled to protect his position. Towards the end of 1941 a new French C-in-C for North Africa was appointed, General Juin. He was firmly controlled by Darlan and Laval. The French army officers were required to sign an oath of allegiance to Pétain.

The Allies saw a way forward – to find a senior Frenchman who could bring French North Africa back into the fold without having to spill blood. One such man was General Giraud, who had gone into hiding near Lyons. Giraud was approached and he attempted to bring key French commanders in North Africa around to his way of thinking. A series of agreements were ironed out and a promise was made to Giraud that he would take over command of the French territories.

It appeared to the French, at least, that the Allies had no intention of making landings in French North Africa. In fact, to a large extent all of the negotiations with Giraud were nothing more than a smoke screen. Operation *Torch* was already well advanced and it would see the first major amphibious landing of the war, and the Americans in particular were keen to play the major role.

The Allies proposed to land 70,000 men between Casablanca and Algiers. This would involve nearly 400 vessels. The landings were aimed to coincide with a major offensive launched by Mont-gomery's 8th Army, which was already pushing Rommel and the remnants of his Afrika Korps back west along the North African coast. Incredibly, a large number of the troops that were to land at Casablanca were actually coming direct from the United States. Additional US troops would land at Oran. The 20,000 or so Anglo-Americans landing at Algiers were to thrust towards Tunisia at the earliest opportunity.

The US 12th Air Force would support the operations around Casablanca and Oran, whilst RAF 133 Group would cover Algiers. Oran was within fighter radius of Gibraltar, but the aircraft would only have a limited amount of fuel, so air cover would be minimal.

It was a risky operation, as the French in North Africa had some-thing in the region of 120,000 men. There were 55,000 troops in Morocco, supported by 160 tanks, 80 armoured cars, anti-aircraft guns and field artillery. The greatest concentrations were around Rabat and the larger ports. The French could also call up the support of around 160 aircraft in Morocco, although across the whole of North Africa they had upwards of 500. They had considerable numbers of Dewoitine 520s and, in any case, the better airfields were in Morocco and were within striking distance of Casablanca. The airfields in Algeria and Tunisia could easily hit the ports. Morocco was believed to have two fighter groups, two reconnaissance groups and four bomber groups. In addition to this there were two *flotilles* of naval aircraft and a pair of transport groups. In Algeria they could deploy three fighter groups, three bomber groups, a recon-naissance group and a *flotille* of naval aircraft. Tunisia boasted one fighter group, one reconnaissance group, a unit of naval flying boats and two bomber groups.

Of even greater concern was the presence of the French navy. There were submarines and destroyers in Bizerta and Oran, along with a crippled battleship. There was a battleship and three cruisers at Dakar and also the prospect of a larger French fleet at Toulon in southern France.

Theoretically, French North Africa was neutral, so there was no blackout. At the time Darlan was in Algiers visiting commanders, dignitaries and military units. At Casablanca, on the evening of 7 November 1942, General Béthouart, Nogués' deputy, had been approached to help overthrow Vichy control of North Africa and ensure that there were no hostilities, at least as far as the Vichy French were concerned. The message he received told him that the landings would take place at 0200 hours on 8 November. He immediately sent off troops to arrest German armistice commis-sions. Officers were sent to Rabat to ensure that the Americans received a warm welcome. He then went with a battalion of troops to occupy army headquarters and even took the step of sending letters to his commanding officer, telling him that the Americans were about to land and that Giraud would assume command. Nogués hesitated; he had taken the precaution of sending out air-craft and submarines, but they had discovered nothing and he believed that his deputy had been duped. There was even talk of his deputy finding himself in front of a firing squad. Then he received word of landings, at around 0500 hours. At first he set them aside as commando raids and ordered his deputy to be placed under arrest on a charge of treason and for French forces to resist the landings.

Thus began the last major battle in which the Vichy French Air Force would take part. There were Vichy squadrons based at Marrakesh, Meknes, Agadir, Casablanca and Rabat. The combined strength was some eighty-six fighters and seventy-eight bombers. Facing them were predominantly F4F Wildcats of the US Navy.

The American pilots found themselves up against determined Frenchmen, many of whom had already seen combat during the battle for France. The Americans, on the other hand, were all untested even though they were proficient pilots. In the American's favour was the performance of their Wildcats, particularly against the Hawk 75As. But the Wildcats were also a match for the better D520s. Lieutenant Charles Shields (VF-41) was pounced on by a pair of D520s but he managed to shoot down the leading French aircraft. Shields then saw three more French aircraft over the airfield. A pair of them were chasing Lieutenant Chuck August's Wildcat and between them Shields and August shot down two Hawks. They strafed the airfield but then Shields, out of ammunition, came up against four more Hawks and was forced to bale out. In horror he saw one of the Hawks aiming to shoot him up whilst he dangled from his parachute. He pulled out his pistol and shot at the aircraft. Shields survived and was taken prisoner, as were some other Wildcat pilots, but their incarceration was only to be brief.

The Wildcats launched attacks on airfields at 0700 hours and caught around nine LeO451 bombers belonging to GBI/22 on the ground, virtually wiping the unit out. At the same time attacks were made on French naval vessels and Wildcats strafed the bombers belonging to GBI/32. Some of these bombers had already been armed and were preparing to take off. During the course of the day several Wildcats were also shot down. By the end of the first day the French had shot down seven US aircraft and had claimed three more probable kills. However, the French Air Force had suffered to an even greater extent, with the loss of thirteen aircraft. It was a fearful first day. During the entire French campaign in 1940, GCII/5 had lost just two pilots but now they were facing annihilation within a matter of days.

Three Douglas DB7 bombers belonging to GBI/32 were also destroyed as they were being rearmed at Casablanca. This left the French unit with just three operational aircraft. Nonetheless, GBI/32, with the support of two other bombers, managed to pull off a bombing mission against US troops at Safi the following morning.

The Vichy forces quickly realized that this was no commando raid, or gentle probe, or even a slow build-up invasion. This was an overwhelming force and the longer they resisted the greater the casualties. On 8 November alone, Allied bombing attacks on French naval vessels had claimed 500 deaths and 1,000 wounded. It was the worst loss since Oran in 1940. The dogfights over Casablanca, although fairly even in terms of casualties, were playing into Allied hands, as French expectation of reinforcement was zero.

By the time Operation *Torch* was into its third day Patton alone, who was in command of the Northern Attack Group, had landed 30,000 troops. But even he was not satisfied with the progress that was being made and drove his men on to make even greater effort. All the French could offer was a token resistance, spearheaded by First World War vintage light tanks. Against them were Shermans and Patton ensured that some of these tanks were spearheading probes into the suburbs of Casablanca by 10 November.

In certain areas French resistance did stiffen, but with the airfields under constant artillery bombardment there was little that the Vichy Air Force could do to help stem the tide. Casualties so far had been relatively low for both sides as far as aircraft were concerned.

GCI/5 had lost four pilots in combat on 9 November, but there was one notable event that day, when Adjutant Bressieux became the last pilot in the Vichy French Air Force to claim a combat victory.

The end for the Vichy Air Force was close and not helped by the fact that thirteen Wildcats had wrecked an airfield at Mediouna, destroying eleven French aircraft. This meant that by the morning of 10 November the Vichy French Air Force in Morocco was down to forty bombers and thirty-seven fighters. On that day two Potez 63-11 reconnaissance aircraft were shot down and Wildcats struck the airfield at Chichaoua, wrecking four more Potez 63-11s.

The combat records of this campaign are fragmentary at best. However, some of the air combats suggest that, at least in the initial stages of the air battle, the Vichy French pilots fought with the same level of vigour as they had in the other theatres of war. Interestingly, many of them would soon be, literally, fighting alongside the very pilots that they were trying to kill.

What we know is that a number of Royal Naval Albacores attacked La Sénia airfield at around dawn on 8 November and in a swirling aerial battle twelve Dewoitine 520s claimed to have shot down four of them and claimed two more as probables. Two of the bombers were claimed by Lieutenant George Blanck (he had already shot down six German aircraft in the Battle of France in 1940). The Dewoitines of GCIII/3 were then set upon by Sea Hurricanes and four of the Vichy aircraft were shot down.

After attacking Tafaroui airfield a number of Seafires of 807 Squadron joined in the fight; they claimed a Dewoitine 520 as well, this being the first ever confirmed kill by a Seafire pilot. One of the Seafires was subsequently shot down by anti-aircraft fire as they made a strafing sweep of La Sénia.

At around 0800 hours a number of Sea Hurricanes belonging to 891 Squadron hit La Sénia and then peeled away, having expended most of their ammunition. At that point, *Sous Lieutenant* Madon in a Dewoitine 520 arrived on the scene and shot one of the Sea Hurricanes down; it was his eighth victory.

It was a confused scene as there were incoming C47s with US paratroopers on board. Their target was La Sénia airfield. They were intercepted by the Dewoitines who were still aloft. The C47s were forced down by the French fighters onto a salt lake some distance from their target. The French then strafed the aircraft on the ground, but the C47s pilots received a message that Tafaroui had been taken and tried to take off and divert there instead. Some of the C47s were unable to take off due to the damage inflicted and the boggy ground.

Later the same morning, the Dewoitines were airborne again and tasked to protect a bombing mission when they were set upon by what they believed to be Hurricanes. They were mistaken as they were Seafires of 807 Squadron. One of the Vichy aircraft was shot down and one of the Dewoitines flown by Sergeant Poupart claimed one of the Seafires in exchange.

The same Seafires were up again that afternoon when they encountered GCIII/3 on their return from escorting a bombing mission. In the ensuing affray *Capitaine* Duval shot down another Seafire to claim his fourth kill.

With Tafaroui in US hands, GCIII/3 strafed the airfield later on in the day. This time they encountered another foe. Flying in from Gibraltar was the US 31st Fighter Group in Spitfires. It was their first ever combat mission and they could be forgiven for mistakenly identifying the Dewoitines as Hurricanes. Soon, they would be sure that the aircraft were not friendlies. *Sous Lieutenant* Pissotte took full advantage by shooting down one of the Spitfires. With the confusion dispelled, the US piloted Spitfires now set about taking the Vichy aircraft to pieces. Commandant Engler and *Capitaine* Mauvier were both shot down and killed and, with his aircraft badly shot up, Sergeant Pouparte baled out.

By the end of the day, the Royal Navy had lost some fifty-three aircraft of all types. Admittedly, not all of these had been lost in air combat or through ground fire; many of the losses were down to insufficient pilot training. Nevertheless, the fight for the skies around Oran was over and the remaining Vichy aircraft were pulled out and redeployed in Morocco.

Over Morocco the situation had been somewhat different. Grumman F4Fs had been prowling the skies since dawn, attacking anything that moved. As some swept over Casablanca half a dozen Curtiss Hawks of GCII/5 took off from Camp Cares. Many of the pilots had seen combat in 1940 and one of them, Lieutenant Pierre Villaceque, had already claimed five kills, all of them German. His sixth kill was a USN OS2U observation aircraft that was directing the fleet gunfire onto targets inland.

At around 0845 hours Commandant Tricaud of GCII/5 took off for a standing patrol. He had shot down five German aircraft in 1940 and had added to his victories with the shooting down of an RAF Wellington off Safi in September 1942. Tricaud, in his Curtiss Hawk, was joined by Lieutenant Abrioux (usually attached to Rabat).

A number of Wildcats of VF-41 had just attacked Camp Cares airfield and had reported seeing some Dewoitine 520s of the unit aloft. They were mistaken as although GCII/5 did have thirteen of the aircraft they could not be used as they had no ammunition for their 20 mm guns. Instead, the Wildcats were engaged by Curtiss Hawks. Initially, it was a slaughter with five of the Vichy pilots killed soon after they had got aloft to intercept the Wildcats, and another two killed as they tried to lift off.

The Wildcats, in short order, had destroyed thirteen of GCII/5's aircraft; amongst the dead were Tricaud and Robert Huvet. Each of the French pilots had managed to take one of the Wildcats with them. Villaceque also shot down one of the Wildcats, but was wounded in the face during the action. Meanwhile, Abrioux zeroed in on a SBD Dauntless and downed it for his sixth victory.

It had been a bad day for VF-9 as well; they had claimed to have shot down a LeO451 off the coast and had, in fact, shot down an

RAF Hudson. This was not uncommon, as on the next day VF-41 shot down an unarmed Spitfire on a photo-reconnaissance mission.

Meanwhile, elsewhere, a negotiated settlement was already in motion. At 0900 hours on 8 November the US *Chargé d'Affaires* to Vichy, Pinkney Tuck, had delivered a letter from President Roosevelt to Pétain:

Washington, D.C., November 8, 1942
White House news release.

MARSHAL PETAIN:
I am sending this message to you as the Chef d'Etat of the United States to the Chef d'Etat of the Republic of France.

When your Government concluded the Armistice Convention in 1940, it was impossible for any of us to foresee the program of systematic plunder which the German Reich would inflict on the French people.

That program, implemented by blackmail and robbery, has deprived the French population of its means of subsistence, its savings; it has paralyzed French industry and transport; it has looted French factories and French farms – all for the benefit of a Nazi Reich and a Fascist Italy under whose Governments no liberty loving nation could long exist.

As an old friend of France and the people of France, my anger and sympathy grows with every passing day when I consider the misery, the want, and the absence from their homes of the flower of French manhood. Germany has neglected no opportunity to demoralize and degrade your great nation.

Today, with greedy eyes on that Empire which France so laboriously constructed, Germany and Italy are proposing to invade and occupy French North Africa in order that they may execute their schemes of domination and conquest over the whole of that continent.

I know you will realize that such a conquest of Africa would not stop there but would be the prelude to further attempts by Germany and Italy to threaten the conquest of large portions of the American Hemisphere, large dominations over the Near and Middle East, and a joining of hands in the Far East with those military leaders of Japan who seek to dominate the whole of the Pacific.

It is evident; of course, that an invasion and occupation of French North and West Africa would constitute for the United States and all of the American Republics the gravest kind of menace to their security – just as it would sound the death knell of the French Empire.

In the light of all the evidence of our enemy's intentions and plans, I have, therefore, decided to dispatch to North Africa powerful American armed forces to cooperate with the governing agencies of Algeria, Tunisia and Morocco in repelling this latest act in the long litany of German and Italian international crime.

These indomitable American forces are equipped with massive and adequate weapons of modern warfare which will be available for your compatriots in North Africa in our mutual fight against the common enemy.

I am making all of this clear to the French Authorities in North Africa, and I am calling on them for their cooperation in repelling Axis threats. My clear purpose is to support and aid the French Authorities and their administrations. That is the immediate aim of these American armies.

I need not tell you that the ultimate and greater aim is the liberation of France and its Empire from the Axis yoke. In so doing we provide automatically for the security of the Americas.

I need not again affirm to you that the United States of America seeks no territories and remembers always the historic friendship and mutual aid which we have so greatly given to each other.

I send to you and, through you, to the people of France my deep hope and belief that we are all of us soon to enter into happier days.

[SIGNED] FRANKLIN D. ROOSEVELT.

But Pétain handed him a reply, which had already been prepared:

It is with stupor and sadness that I learned tonight of the aggression of your troops against North Africa.

I have read your message. You invoke pretexts which nothing justifies. You attribute to your enemies intentions which have not ever been manifested in acts. I have always declared that we would defend our empire if it were attacked; you should know that we would defend it against any aggressor whoever it might be. You should know that I would keep my word.

In our misfortune I had, when requesting the armistice, protected our empire and it is you who, acting in the name of a country to which so many memories and ties bind us, have taken such a cruel initiative.

France and her honor are at stake.

We are attacked; we shall defend ourselves; this is the order I am giving.

[SIGNED] PHILIPPE PETAIN

Aerial combat continued on 9 November. Over Casablanca, five aircraft of GCII/5 chanced a ground attack on landing craft at dawn and were extremely lucky to get away with minor damage. The USN had decided to put up standing patrols of Wildcats to cover the fleet. About an hour later a mixed group of Vichy bombers from the air force and the navy came over for another attack. They were escorted by some fifteen Curtiss Hawks of GCII/5. The Wildcats pounced from a higher altitude on the formations.

In the ensuing battle four of the Hawks were shot down, two of the pilots were killed, *Adjutant Chef* Georges Tesseraud was wounded and another pilot baled out. Lieutenant Camille Plubeau's aircraft was badly shot up and his landing gear was damaged; he managed to survive the forced landing back at Rabat. Plubeau had managed fourteen kills and four probable hits in the Battle of France in 1940.

Ensign Gerhardt, flying one of VF-41 Wildcats, was shot down by *Sergeant Chef* Bressieux. It was Bressieux's ninth victory of the war. Gerhardt was lucky and survived unhurt. It was the only Vichy victory of the day.

Whilst GCII/5 was fighting for its life in the skies, other US aircraft were punishing the airfields and smashing up any Vichy aircraft still on the ground. It was becoming increasingly obvious that resistance in the air was coming to an end.

Only a few hours later, Laval accepted German assistance. It would begin with air support and, subsequently, additional ground forces. Darlan, meanwhile, had issued orders to French troops and naval vessels in the Oran and Casablanca area to ceasefire. He also authorized Juin to arrange a settlement to cover the whole of North Africa and agreed that control of Algiers would be transferred to the Americans at 2000 hours. They would also be granted use of Algiers harbour the following morning. Additional negotiations took place on 9 November and, after protracted arguments, Darlan gave in to an ultimatum; the order to ceasefire was sent out at 1120 hours.

Pétain approved the arrangements, but Laval immediately called him and convinced him to change his mind. Darlan was now in a quandary and said: 'There is nothing I can do but revoke the order I signed this morning.'

The chief negotiator, General Mark Clark, who was also in overall command of Operation *Torch*, replied: 'You will do nothing of the kind. There will be no revocation of these orders; and, to make it certain, I shall hold you in custody.'

By 10 November, the Vichy Air Force was pinned down, what remained of the units had been withdrawn to Meknes. The air was thick with enemy aircraft, hitting airfields and other ground targets at will. There was little the Vichy pilots could do to help.

As a direct result of the ceasefire agreement the Germans chose to occupy southern France. German mechanized units, supported by six Italian divisions, moved in. Meanwhile, German aircraft began arriving near Tunis. From 11 November 1942 the airlift began to accelerate. Local French troops were disarmed and, by the end of the month, 100 German tanks and 15,000 infantry had arrived, along with 9,000 Italians.

There still remained the difficulty of the French fleet, which was in Toulon, yet Darlan had switched sides. Darlan had been promised control of the fleet, but as the German troops began pouring into Vichy France it had become clear that even the Vichy French would not countenance their vessels falling into German hands. Negotiations had taken place on 11 November between the Vichy French and the Germans. The settlement had agreed that Toulon should remain under Vichy control but German and Italian troops surrounded the port and urgent negotiations and planning took place with Pétain at the centre. The Germans had already planned Operation *Lila*, which was to be carried out by the 7th Panzer Division and other units. It focused on preventing the scuttling of the French fleet. Operation *Lila* was given the go ahead on 19 November. It would be executed on 27 November 1942.

German units entered Toulon at 0400 hours and met with limited resistance. The Germans broke into the fleet headquarters at 0430 hours, arresting key naval personnel. But there was sufficient time to transmit the scuttling order to Admiral Laborde, on board the flagship *Strasbourg*. Shortly before 0500 hours, German troops had also entered the arsenal and had begun firing on French vessels to prevent unauthorized movement. Fighting broke out and the Germans demanded that the vessels be surrendered.

The *Strasbourg* went down first, followed by *Colbert*. Further vessels sank as the German troops attempted to clamber on board. Nonetheless, scuttling charges wrecked vessels across the fleet, including the destroyers and submarines. Over the course of a short period of time the French destroyed seventy-seven of their own vessels. All that the Germans could salvage were three disarmed destroyers, three merchant ships, four partially wrecked submarines and two cannibalized old battleships. Subsequently, the Italians were able to salvage some of the cruisers, but they would never see action.

Darlan had been controversially appointed High Commissioner for French North and West Africa on 14 November 1942. He was in his headquarters in Algiers on the afternoon of 24 December 1942. Emmanuel d'Astier walked in and shot him twice. Darlan's assassination at least solved a problem, as undoubtedly he would have been a key opponent to de Gaulle. But Darlan had already served his useful purpose. If the Allies had not succeeded in getting him onside then Operation *Torch* could well have been far bloodier than it had been. Churchill described the assassination as being both criminal but also something of a relief. It relieved the allies of any embarrassment of having to deal with him. General Mark Clark saw the death as very timely. Whilst he regretted the way in which Darlan had died, he recognised that Darlan had served his purpose and that his death actually solved some potential problems, particularly as to Darlan's position in the future. Darlan was replaced by Giraud, who organised the rapid court martial of the assassin. He had him executed on 26 December 1942.

Chapter Eight

Flying for the *Luftwaffe*

In the earlier stages of the war the Germans had an extremely negative attitude towards foreigners serving in the armed forces. Notable exceptions were those considered to be Germanic. This essentially meant those from Flanders, the Netherlands and from Scandinavia. These men were generally assigned to the *Waffen* SS.

To a larger extent the question of foreigners in the armed forces presented difficult decisions for Germany. On the one hand, there were many groups that were not considered to be racially acceptable. On the other, if conquered countries provided manpower the point might come when those countries demanded concessions from Germany on the basis that their men had already contributed towards Germany's ultimate victory.

For many key German politicians and members of the armed forces the question was somewhat simpler to answer. At this stage of the war, having successfully annexed portions of Poland and Czechoslovakia and having achieved union with Austria, Germany did not need them to supplement the manpower. As the war progressed and expanded, Germany began to take the more pragmatic view that certain nationalities could make a valuable contribution. After all, there were well trained soldiers, naval personnel and pilots that had belonged to conquered races languishing without a role, yet willing to contribute.

By 1941 Germany had recruited French, Belgians, Spaniards and Croats. Later, the Germans would welcome Russians, Indians, Tunisians, Ukrainians, Serbs and Vietnamese.

Despite this, the fundamental ideological reservations remained. This is exemplified by a speech made by *Generaloberst* Jodl (Chief of the Operations Staff of the German Armed Forces) on 7 November

1943: 'But the drawing upon foreign nationals as fighting soldiers must be viewed with great caution and scepticism.'

Paradoxically, many of the foreign nationals joined the German armed forces after the tide had turned against Germany. There were huge numbers in the *Waffen* SS, as well as the *Wehrmacht* (regular German army). The *Kriegsmarine* (German navy) had a fair number too, but for the most part the *Luftwaffe* had restricted its recruitment of foreigners to provide manpower for anti-aircraft batteries. The *Luftwaffe* felt, and with some justification, that if a pilot from a conquered country was given an expensive piece of equipment he would simply fly the aircraft to the nearest enemy airfield and switch sides.

This cautious scepticism had not been the case in the last great conflict, before the outbreak of the Second World War. In Spain during the civil war both the Republicans and the Nationalists had used foreign aircrew and pilots. A mix of adventurers, idealists and a fair few mercenaries, led by the Frenchman André Malroux, had served in the *Escuadrilla España* for the government in Madrid. Many foreigners flew for the Nationalists, mostly Portuguese. In fact, the German-built Ju52S and the Italian-made SM79S of the *Missão Militar de Observação* were flown by Portuguese.

Even later, in the winter war between the Russians and the Finns in 1939 to 1940, at least 200 foreign aircrews had volunteered for service in the Finnish *Suomen Illmavoimat*, and even Swedes had served in the F19 volunteer squadrons. Russia had its own foreign pilots, including Czechs in fighters, Latvians flying night bombers and the Normandie-Niemen French fighter regiment. Offers from foreign nationals had not been met with rejection by the RAF either. Indeed, in the dark days of the Battle of Britain the RAF had been desperate for trained pilots to replace the ruinous losses from the Battle of France and to cope with the attrition caused by day and night *Luftwaffe* attacks on Britain throughout the summer and autumn of 1940. The RAF had willingly embraced French, Greeks, Yugoslavs, Czechs, Belgians, Dutch and Norwegians. All of them made telling contributions to the air war.

Regardless of the *Luftwaffe*'s unwillingness to actively recruit foreign pilots and aircrew, it is estimated that by 1943 to 1944 at least 100 foreigners were serving in this capacity in the *Luftwaffe*, from a solitary Brazilian of German descent to Spaniards, Russians, Estonians, Latvians, Norwegians, Czechs, Croats, Danes, Italians, Dutch, Belgians and men from Alsace-Lorraine. Most of the instances were still isolated cases; there were no plans to group the nationalities together to form complete foreign units. This was probably a great mistake and a missed opportunity for the Germans. Had they created distinct foreign units no doubt they would have been excellent propaganda tools and effective recruitment models.

By May 1944 the *Luftwaffe* had enormous numbers of foreign nationals in their ranks. This led to the creation of the post of General for Foreign Personnel, as head of a new department. The first incumbent was *Generalleutant* Grosch and later *General der Flieger* Julius Schulz. The role was designed to represent the foreign nationals with the exception of the eastern recruits and volunteers. These men were handled by *Generalleutant* Heinrich Aschenbrenner (the Inspector for Foreign Personnel). By December 1944 its role came under the control of the Chief of the General Staff of the *Luftwaffe*.

Many of the recruits (a mix of volunteers, auxiliaries, former soldiers, prisoners of war and deserters) joined as they were fundamentally anti-Bolshevik. The men saw the worsening situation for Germany as a battle they needed to fight in order to stave off the threat of Soviet domination of Europe. As the war progressed the training schedules for pilots and aircrew were drastically cut from 210 flying hours in 1942 to around 160 hours by 1944. In fact, by the middle of 1944, *Luftwaffe* losses were mounting to unsustainable levels. On average, a *Luftwaffe* pilot had a 50 per cent chance of being shot down before he had even flown ten sorties.

For a large number of the men, particularly in the annexed areas of Europe, they were obliged to serve in the German military. A role, in fact any role in the *Luftwaffe*, was deemed to be a distinctly better option than finding themselves fighting for their lives on the crumbling Eastern Front. As far as the French serving in the *Luftwaffe* were concerned, the decision was a far more ideological one than a choice between a softer option with the *Luftwaffe* or a brutally short existence fighting against the Russians. Soon after the Germans launched Operation *Barbarossa* against Russia in June 1941, a French voluntary legion was created. It was known as the *Légion des Volontaires Français* (LVF).

The group was based in Paris and headed up by the collaborator Pierre Costantini. Costantini was a former First World War pilot, violently anti-British and the leader and founder of the *Ligue Français*. He also planned to create a separate Aviation League (*Légion des Aviateurs Français*).

Considerable numbers of French pilots and aircrew volunteered. On 7 July 1941 Otto Abetz, the German ambassador in Paris, wrote to the Berlin-based German Foreign Ministry: 'The number of trained airmen who have put down their names for the LVF has increased to fifty, including thirty well known bomber pilots.'

On 1 November 1941 the LVF moved into a permanent head-quarters in the former British Railways building at Rue Godot de Mauroy in Paris. Costantini would be disappointed by the German reaction to the Frenchmen rallying to National Socialism; they were not supportive of a French aviation contribution. Undeterred, Costantini, along with Captain Caêl, set up flight-training courses. It was to no avail; instead, by 1942 the National Socialist Motor Corps (NSKK) was operating out of the building. They were recruiting drivers for the *Luftwaffe*. Seven companies were created and other men would serve in a ground role against partisans in Italy. Following the disbandment of Vichy armed forces, the Germans were keen to transfer French airmen directly into the *Luftwaffe en bloc*, but in a non-flying capacity.

The German High Command War Diary, dated 27 November 1942, noted:

> On request of the *Luftwaffe*, the *Führer* has declared that personnel from the disbanded formations of the French armed forces can at once be taken over for service in the German armed forces, preferably for air defence reporting tasks, in AA artillery and coastal artillery; the men are to be put up and looked after according to the pre-war French conditions and put under German military law.

This command had, however, arrived too late. *Luftwaffe* Operations Staff received a report from *Luftflotte* 3 on 29 November 1942: 'The demobilization of the French air force had already taken place so quickly that the servicemen could not be taken over for the German service use.'

Some Frenchmen were determined to serve with the *Luftwaffe* despite all of the hurdles. The Vichy Government had ordered 225 Loiré et Olivier 451 aircraft in August 1941. This was with full German agreement. After the German occupation of all of France in November 1942, another thirty transport versions of the aircraft, the 451T, were completed.

By 1943 a French-crewed transport squadron had been established. It was known as the Hansa Transport Squadron. Elsewhere, a fair number of 451 aircraft served with the *Luftwaffe*'s IV/TG4 (in fact, as of March 1944 110 of these aircraft were on the *Luftwaffe*'s books, with around seventy-three of them operational). Many of the transport flights, particularly in France, were handled by French personnel. By the summer of 1944, the IV/TG4 was disbanded and the aircraft and their crews were transferred to the Hansa squadron. Initially, there were plans for there to be nine full French crews, with supporting mechanics.

Even after the Normandy landings in June 1944, these Frenchmen were still serving with the *Luftwaffe*. Some were French pilots and crews that had been trained in Germany; others were former Vichy crew, whilst another group had flown with Air France. A German order dated 18 September 1944, recognising Allied air superiority in France, led to the Hansa squadron being disbanded.

Prior to the outbreak of the Second World War, Air France had used the Bloch MB200 monoplane on its short-haul European network. It could carry sixteen passengers. By 1944 Lufthansa had taken all of the remaining Bloch MB200s to replenish its losses. Lufthansa had leased eleven of these aircraft as early as November 1942. Lufthansa had lost a great deal of aircraft during the war. There were conventional losses from having aircraft shot down, but the majority were requisitioned and most of what remained did not have sufficient spares to keep them airworthy. In fact, the Lufthansa air fleet had shrunk from 151 aircraft in early 1939 to just forty-seven by the end of 1943. Despite the fact that the Bloch MB200 was not that reliable, ten were still in service by the end of June 1944.

The annexation of Alsace and Lorraine meant that from 1942 the male population there was expected to serve in the German armed forces. A large number of the affected men had simply melted away. Some had fled to find refuge in Switzerland; others had disappeared into unoccupied France; others were lying low with relatives and friends, in the hope that they would never be found. For others who found themselves recruited by the Germans the experiences and approach of the men was markedly different. Some actively embraced National Socialism; others took a more pragmatic view that sooner or later they would be mobilized. It was better to volunteer; at least that offered the opportunity to choose the branch of service, rather than being posted. Clearly, the *Luftwaffe* was the best option, followed by the *Kriegsmarine* and a last resort was the *Wehrmacht*.

Charles Kern was born in Alsace in 1924. His father worked for the German Civil Administration and had warned him that following annexation all men in Alsace would be liable for conscription. Charles Kern was already a member of the Aviation Hitler Youth (*Flieger* HJ) and as such he volunteered to become an officer in the *Luftwaffe* in 1941. He spent the next two years in training, by which time his father's prediction had been proved correct. By September 1943 he was a lieutenant and had been posted to 2/NJG4, operating out of Laon-Athies. At the beginning of 1944 he flew his first operational sortie. On 30 May 1944, having taken off from Florenne in Belgium, he shot down one of the United States Air Force's 801st Bomber Group's B24 Liberators. On 17 June 1944, flying his Ju88 over the English Channel, he had engine problems. Kern managed to nurse the aircraft back towards Laon-Athies and here he was ambushed by an RAF Mosquito. Kern's Ju88 was shot down, all of his crew were killed and Kern was badly scarred with burns.

At the end of the war Kern, then at Eggebek in Schleswig-Holstein, was captured by the Allies. He was released on 19 January 1946 and headed home. For his collaboration he was sentenced to five years' hard labour and ten years of exile from Alsace, which was once again French.

The other side of the coin is the story of René Darbois. His experiences proved the Germans' worst fears about letting conquered foreign nationals fly their aircraft. Darbois was also born in 1924. He attended basic training at Oschatz and then Officer Candidate

School (*Luftkriegsshule* 7) at Tulln, close to Vienna in Austria. He undertook more pilot training with JG103 (at Chatereau and Orleans) until May 1944. After that he was sent for further training at Stargard in Pomerania with the Replacement Fighter Wing belonging to Replacement Group West.

On 25 June 1944 he was piloting an Bf109G on a ferry flight from Maniago to Ghedi in Italy. Darbois had never seen active service. Maintaining radio silence as instructed, Darbois indicated to one of his colleagues that he was feeling unwell and was returning to base. He pulled away from the formation of fifteen other Bf109s. When he was out of sight he climbed to 26,000 feet and made for the south. He landed behind Allied lines at Santa Maria and surrendered himself. From the outset he maintained that it had always been his intention to desert at the first opportunity.

To prove himself loyal to the Allies and to a Free France he volunteered to fly with the de Gaulle *Groupe de Chasse Corse*. He adopted the false name of Guyot in case he was shot down and captured by the Germans after having baled out over enemy territory. Had this happened then the Germans would have realized his true identity and Darbois would, undoubtedly, have been executed as a deserter.

Chapter Nine

Pilots and Aircraft

Pilots

Information on the pilots of the Vichy Air Force is scant and fragmentary, with much of the research focussing on their exploits in June 1940 and in some cases skipping two or three years until they returned to the Allied fold.

Yet there are some where more than snippets of information have been uncovered, not least of which is Pierre Le Gloan, who appears to have been one of those men who had a natural flying talent. He was just nineteen when he gained his wings in 1932. He was already an *adjutant chef* in the *5e Escadrille* of *Groupe de Chasse* III/6 at the outbreak of the war. Initially, he flew Morane 406 aircraft out of Chartres as part of the air defence of Paris.

He claimed his first (joint) kill on 23 November 1939 when he was involved in the shooting down of a Dornier near Verdun. He claimed a second on 2 March 1940. He managed to add two He111s to his total before his unit was transferred down to Luc in the South of France. Here, they were issued with Dewoitine 520s in readiness for the Italian invasion.

On 13 June 1940, he shared two Fiat BR20 bombers with another pilot, but his most famous exploit of this phase of the war was yet to come. On 15 June he was on patrol with other aircraft of the squadron when they intercepted a force of Italian bombers escorted by a number of Fiat CR42 fighters. In the space of the next forty-five minutes Le Gloan shot down four of the fighters and one of the BR20 bombers. He was immediately promoted to *sous lieutenant*.

After the fall of France, his unit, GCIII/6, was transferred to Algiers and then on to Syria. By mid-July 1941 he had brought his total up to eighteen, which included five RAF Hurricanes and a Gladiator. After the Vichy surrender, Le Gloan joined the Free

French and became the commander of *3e Escadrille* 'Rousillon' on 11 August 1943. They were equipped with Bell P39N Airacobras and used for coastal patrols.

On a patrol on 11 September, black smoke was belching out of Le Gloan's aircraft engine. It then stopped and he tried to glide down to make a belly landing on the water. The mechanism to release his drop tank failed and when the aircraft hit the water it exploded, killing Le Gloan.

Pierre Boillot gained his wings at the age of twenty on 7 July 1938. He joined the 4th *Escadrille* of GCII/7 in May 1939 and was based at Luxeuil at the outbreak of the war. He flew escort missions for reconnaissance aircraft in his Morane 406. He encountered his first enemy aircraft, a Do17, in November, but failed to shoot it down. His first victory came on the morning of 20 April 1940 when he shot down a Bf109 over Belfort. On 10 May, he shared a victory with another pilot when they shot down an He111. On 11 May he added to his score with a Ju88. This was followed in June by another He111 and a Do17.

Soon afterwards, GCII/7 was transferred to North Africa and equipped with Dewoitine 520s. Here, Boillot remained until November 1942 when he took the opportunity to join the Free French after the Operation *Torch* landings. He would go on to shoot down two Italian Maachi 202s and a Bf109. By September 1942, he was a *sergeant chef* and involved in the invasion of Corsica. Here, he flew in support of Operation *Dragoon*, the Allied invasion of Southern France. In October, Boillot added a pair of Ju88s to his record, which he shot down into the sea off Aljaccio. He was soon promoted to *sous lieutenant* and throughout late 1944 and into 1945 he added four more Bf109s to his tally. He ended the war with thirteen confirmed kills and one probable.

At the age of twenty Michel Madon joined the French Air Force in 1938. He was posted to GCI/3 at Cannes in February 1940. The unit was in the process of being upgraded from the Morane 406s to Dewoitine 520s. As a *sous lieutenant*, Maldon left with his unit bound for Suippes on 13 May 1940 to take part in the Battle of France in their new fighters. Within a matter of hours they were engaged in aerial duels over the River Meuse, giving Maldon the opportunity to claim his first kill, a Bf110.

Between 6 and 16 June 1940, Madon added two Hs126s, a Do17 and an Me109 to his score. He also had two probable hits. On 18 June, the squadron retired to Oran and then to Tunisia. On 10 November 1941 he was given command of the 1st *Escadrille* of the squadron. Madon did not see action for a year, but following the Operation *Torch* landings in November 1942, he added a Sea Hurricane and two or three C47s to his tally.

Madon opted to throw his lot in with the Allies and was assigned to GCII/7 in April 1943 and then in the September to GCI/7 where he flew Spitfires. He scored a probable Do17 kill on 26 November 1943 and damaged a pair of Focke-Wulf 200s. He was now on eleven confirmed and four probable hits.

Madon was involved in the liberation of Corsica and later, on 2 June 1944, his aircraft suffered engine failure over Italy. Rather than bale out over land and become a prisoner of war, Madon opted to bale out over the sea. By all accounts he had been lucky to have been found.

Léon Richard gained his wings at the age of nineteen, in 1929. He became a non-commissioned officer in 1933 and completed all of his flight training in July 1935. In November 1937 he commanded an Algerian-based reconnaissance unit, GAR571. For a short period of time, in April 1940, Richard commanded the 1st *Escadrille* of GCI/9 before he was then posted, along with his unit, to Tunisia in the beginning of May that year.

By the end of August 1940, now flying Dewoitine 520s, Richard commanded the 6th *Escadrille* of GCIII/6 in Syria. On 8 June 1941 he shot down a Royal Navy Fairey Fulmar and the following day he claimed a Hurricane. On 13 June he shot down a Blenheim belonging to 11 Squadron and added to this score on 23 June, when he shot down both a Tomahawk and a Hurricane. Richard's last kill in Syria was on 5 July, when he shot down another Hurricane. After that, the unit returned to Algeria.

Richard claimed his seventh and final victory on 18 May 1942, when he shot down a Royal Navy Fairey Fulmar. After the Operation *Torch* landings Richard joined the Free French, but was on a training flight on 26 May 1943 when he ran out of fuel. He was killed when he force-landed in North Africa.

George Blanck joined the French Air Force at the age of twenty-one and graduated from officer school in November 1939. He was involved in the defence of Algeria, where he shot down a pair of, presumably, Seafires or Sea Hurricanes, both on 8 November 1942. He was also credited with the destruction of three C47s. During the Battle of France he had claimed two Bf109s, two HS126s, a He111 and a Ju87. During this battle he had been assigned to GCI/3, flying Dewoitine 520s.

By the time the Operation *Torch* landings took place George Blanck was with GCIII/3. Following the surrender of Vichy forces in North Africa he was involved in the liberation of Corsica and on 30 September 1943 he shot down a Me323, near the Isle of Elba in his Spitfire.

Louis Delfino is an interesting case. His father had been killed in the First World War when Delfino was relatively young, but his lack of funding had not prevented him from graduating from Saint-Cyr in September 1933. Delfino joined the French Air Force and received his wings on 27 July 1934. By 1938 he had joined GCI/4, based at Rheims.

Delfino was by now a *capitaine* and the adjutant of the group. His unit moved to Dunkirk-Mardyck on 10 May 1940. No fewer than eight pilots of GCI/4 shared the shooting down of a He111 on the following day. On the same day Delfino scored a probable kill on a Bf109 and did the same two days later.

On 17 May he took over command of the 4th *Escadrille* of GCII/9, flying Bloch 152s. Delfino managed to shoot down a Bf109 and a HS126 on 26 May then, over the course of the period 5 to 10 June he shot down three HS126s, a Do17 and a He111 in the defence of Paris.

Delfino was posted to GCI/4 again in June 1942 and was stationed at Dakar. On 12 August he took part in the shooting down of an RAF Wellington off Dakar. After the surrender of Vichy North Africa, Delfino joined the Free French and, as part of GCI/4, was equipped with Martin Marylands to carry out coastal patrol duties. Delfino was not happy with this arrangement and so on 11 January 1944 he joined the French unit known as *Normandie Niémen*. This was a French unit that fought alongside the Russian Air Force.

Delfino arrived in Russia on 28 February 1944 and was assigned to use the Yak3. He was involved in the offensive in East Prussia and on 16 October he shot down a Bf109 and claimed a Focke-Wulf 190 as a probable. Just a week later he claimed two more of these aircraft and later in the month he also claimed another Fw190 and a probable Bf109.

On 12 November Delfino was promoted to become second in command of the unit and by the end of the Second World War he had not only been promoted to lieutenant-colonel, but had also shot down another four German aircraft.

Marcel Albert joined the French Air Force in May 1938 and by February 1940 he was in GCI/3, flying Dewoitine 520s. His squadron was deployed to Rheims in May 1940 and on 14 May he shot down a Do17 and then a Bf109, the latter only being a probable. Before the end of the armistice he also claimed a probable He111.

Albert remained with the squadron in Algeria and was involved in missions largely escorting bomber raids against Gibraltar. However, on 14 October 1941 he escaped with Marcel Lefèvre to Gibraltar and switched sides, joining No. 340 Squadron and flying in Spitfires. He subsequently flew forty-seven missions over Northern France.

Albert joined the group of French pilots flying Yak fighters in Russia and on 16 June 1943 he claimed his first kill, a Fw189, in his Yak1. By July he was flying Yak9s and this is when his tally began to accelerate. Between July 1943 and October of the same year he claimed thirteen, although some of these kills were uncertain. Albert was flying Yak3s by mid-October 1944, adding eight more kills to his tally by the end of the month.

There is some considerable dispute as to the number of kills that Albert managed to achieve. He may have had twenty-three confirmed and two probable hits, but it is difficult to be certain as records are incomplete.

Another interesting case was that of Camille Plubeau. He had joined the French Air Force in 1929 and by October 1930 was a sergeant. On 16 May 1939 GCII/4 was being formed and, now as an adjutant, Plubeau joined the unit, being promoted to *sous lieutenant* on 16 March 1940.

Plubeau was flying a Curtiss Hawk on 18 May 1940, escorting a formation of Potez 63-11s in the Ardennes sector. He saw a He126 and reported the sighting. The French pilots had dubbed this aircraft 'The Dragonfly' and for the French ground troops it was known as 'The Informer'. As soon as the German pilot knew he had been seen he turned into a dive and made for the German lines. But he was too late; another patrol (call sign Red Devils) attacked the He126 and saw it crash in flames on the bank of the River Aisne. It hit the ground with such impact that there was burning debris on the opposite side of the river. The Red Devils then regrouped and took up a position underneath Plubeau and his formation. Suddenly four Me109s appeared, emerging from the clouds to the north and only 200m from Plubeau. The Germans did not see the French aircraft and Plubeau then ordered the formation to head home, with his own aircraft aiming to protect the formation. More Me109s appeared and Plubeau shot one down, as did Captain Engler. The French then regrouped once again. The Red Devils seemed to have disappeared, but then Plubeau spotted five aircraft ahead of him. Unfortunately they were more Me109s and as they were above Plubeau he signalled to enter a shallow dive into clouds. The Me109s passed by. The French formation then began to climb again. It was a tense situation and Plubeau feared that at any moment they could come under enemy attack. The Red Devils reappeared and the two formations continued to climb. When they were at around 2500m the French spotted thirty He111s in formation flying from the west. Plubeau remained with his formation whilst the Red Devils engaged. Plubeau watched carefully for German fighters and seeing none he and his other Curtiss Hawks joined in the attack. Plubeau himself had problems chasing the German bombers, as he was suffering from engine problems. He was now around 250m behind the German formation and opened fire, seeing one of the He111s belching smoke. The enemy aircraft dropped out of formation and went into a dive. Plubeau then attacked a second German aircraft and saw it begin to burst into flames. His wing man and two other aircraft fired on the same aircraft, finishing it off. By now the Curtiss Hawks were running short of ammunition and fuel and there were only four of them able to continue to fight with the He111s. Plubeau saw a second formation of German bombers, escorted by fighters, heading towards them from the northwest. He signalled to break off, but one of the Curtiss aircraft was too heavily engaged. Belatedly the aircraft did break off, but by then the Me109s were closing in on Plubeau and the other pilots. Plubeau fired his machine guns to help Engler to escape but to his horror a Me109 turned straight in front of him, just 150m away. Instinctively Plubeau opened fire and shot it down. The French were now in a serious position, particularly Plubeau, whose engine was really struggling, but nonetheless he managed to break off and get back to base.

The account of the engagement is confirmed in German records. The Bf109s belonged to 7/JG53 and the aircraft lost was flown by *Obertleutnant* Wolf-Dietrich Wilcke. According to Wilcke's own journal, *Oberfeldwebel* Frans Götz was also shot down. They were both taken prisoner, but later rejoined their unit.

Following the armistice Plubeau left to join GCII/5 in Tunisia and was involved in the Tunisian campaign, but did not claim any victories. He later became commander of GCII/9 on 20 November 1944. Plubeau had fourteen confirmed air victories, eight of which were his own and not shared.

Edmond Marin la Meslée joined the French Air Force in 1931 and by October 1937, with the rank of *sous leutenant*, was assigned to GCI/5. He was spectacularly successful as a Curtiss Hawk fighter pilot, downing five He111s, four HS126s, three Ju87s, a Ju88, a Do17, a Do215 and a Bf109.

On 25 June 1940 GCI/5 moved to the South of France and then in August 1940 to Rabat in Morocco. La Meslée played a very minor role in resisting the invasion of French North Africa in November 1942. In September 1943 his group left for Tafaraoui to be issued with P40s and P39s. Ultimately, they were to fly P47s, in October 1944. He was back fighting over French soil by September 1944, carrying out strafing missions.

On 29 December the group moved closer to the front and on 4 February 1945 he took part in a three aircraft patrol. They attacked a temporary bridge at Neuf Brisach and he spotted a column of German trucks so flew down to strafe the convoy. His aircraft was hit by anti-aircraft fire and it crash-landed, killing la Meslée when it exploded.

Gabriel Gauthier was assigned to GCII/7 in October 1938. He was severely wounded on 21 December 1939, but still managed to land his aircraft safely, despite the fact that he was partially paralyzed. He rejoined his unit in June 1940 in Tunisia and spent a relatively uneventful time until November 1942.

GCII/7 was one of the first units to be re-equipped with Spitfires and Gauthier took part in the last stages of the Tunisian campaign in April 1942. He was shot down over France on 15 September 1944 and, although wounded, he made contact with the resistance and escaped to Switzerland, rejoining his unit and becoming the commander on 24 February 1945.

During the course of his Second World War military service Gauthier had downed a Do17 and a Bf109 in November and December 1939 and then he had seen a long gap until, once again, he was in combat with German aircraft. He shot down a Do217, two Ju88s and four Bf109s between 30 September 1943 and 14 April 1945.

Georges Tricaud enlisted in the aviation branch of the French army in January 1921. By October 1926 he was a *sous leutenant* and by 1939 he had taken command of GCI/6, gradually gaining pro-motions until he took command of GCIII/9 in August 1940.

During the battle of France, as a *capitaine* with GCI/6 and flying a Bloch MB152, Tricaud shot down a Ju52 on 7 April 1940. In the following month, over the course of two days from 20 May, he shot down a Bf109 and then a Do17.

After the fall of France he remained with the unit and on 8 November 1942 his aircraft was involved in a dogfight against Grumman Wildcats of VF-41 in Morocco. It is believed that he managed to shoot down two of the Wildcats before being shot down and killed himself.

Aircraft

The French Air Force became an independent branch of the armed services on 2 July 1934. In the previous year a programme had been set in motion to set up a production plan for new military aircraft. It was to call for something in the region of 1,400 new aircraft to be built as an immediate priority. This included 350 fighters. Already, there were promising aircraft coming through, but some of these were still very much on the drawing board.

With the reoccupation of the Rhineland in March 1936 the French Government realized that they would have to accelerate their re-equipping of the armed forces. The plan called for the French Air Force to be doubled by the end of 1939. Out of the 1,554 aircraft, some 378 were fighters. Within fourteen months, between November 1938 and December 1939, the French aircraft industry itself built 936 combat aircraft, including 273 fighters. This low figure was largely as a result of political unrest and the fact that the aircraft industry had been nationalized in August 1936.

By January 1938 the most advanced of the air force's 793 fighters were the fifty-four Dewoitine 510s, which had fixed landing gear.

French intelligence estimated that the *Luftwaffe*, by the beginning of 1938, had some 2,850 aircraft on strength and this included 850 modern fighters. This set the French Government a wholly new target, which was to give priority to aircraft production. A new plan was approved in March 1938. The French Air Force would have a strength of some 2,617 aircraft, including 1,081 fighters. It was believed that this would be enough to create thirty-two *groupes de chasse* (GC or fighter groups), along with sixteen local defence squadrons.

However, the plans that were due for completion within three years, were entirely disrupted when France declared war on Germany following its invasion of Poland in September 1939. This left the French Air Force in a difficult position of trying to prepare for war against a backdrop of reduced aircraft production and constant changes in priorities.

One of the common aircraft that was used by both the French Air Force, and ultimately the Vichy Air Force, was the Morane Saulnier 406. The production of this aircraft had begun in 1934 and, despite a series of setbacks, the first fifty production aircraft were contracted in April 1937. A second order was placed in the August for another eighty.

The deteriorating political situation by April 1938 prompted the Air Ministry to order an additional 825 of these aircraft, and production steadily increased to six aircraft a day by April 1939. The MS406 production officially ended in March 1940.

Equipped with auxiliary fuel tanks, the aircraft had a maximum range of just over 930 miles. But only a limited number of these external tanks had been ordered. Some of them would be fitted onto MS406s, which were subsequently ferried to Syria in June 1941.

The MS406 had a maximum range of 302 mph. It was armed with a propeller shaft-mounted 20 mm canon with only sixty rounds. It also had two 7.5 mm machine guns with thirty rounds each on the wings. Without the auxiliary tanks it had a range of just over 620 miles.

On 10 May 1940, when German forces invaded Belgium and the Netherlands, there were theoretically 313 MS406s assigned to ten GC units in mainland France. However, only 163 of them were serviceable; the other 150 had mechanical problems. There was also supposed to be another 527 allotted to the French Air Force. But of this total 145 were being used for pilot training or were in local defence fighter groups, 136 were being stored, 111 were being repaired, and 135 were either in Syria, North Africa or Corsica. In fact, by this date the manufacturers had delivered 1,074. The French Air Force was in the process of converting the units that had been given MS406s into squadrons with the newer Bloch 152s, or the Dewoitine 520s.

Around 300 MS406s were lost during the Battle of France. Around 150 of these were actually shot down either by German aircraft or by anti-aircraft fire. Around fifty were shot down by small arms fire when attacking armoured formations. The other 150 were either lost due to accidents or were unserviceable when the order to evacuate the airfield was given, meaning that the crews destroyed them. Of the 144 French fighter pilots that were killed during the battle of France, some seventy-five of them were MS406 pilots.

Once the armistice had been signed three fighter groups in North Africa and one in Syria were using MS406s. All of the groups apart from GCI/7 at Rayak were disbanded between July and August 1940.

The history of the Bloch 152 dates back to its original incarnation in 1934, the Bloch 150. It was being designed and tested at the same time as the development of the MS406 and it was clear that the Air Ministry preferred the MS406.

The initial order for the Bloch 151 was for 475 aircraft, but this was reduced to 432 in April 1938. The first 144 were considered somewhat underpowered and, consequently, the remaining 288 were given upgraded engines and re-designated Bloch 152s.

Component shortages resulted in sixty-one of the aircraft not being completed. The first Bloch 152 was delivered to the French Air Force on 7 March 1939. By the time war broke out, 123 of the aircraft had entered service. There were many problems with spare parts and basic engineering difficulties. This meant that on 10 May 1940, when the battle of France began, there were only 140 Bloch 151s and 363 Bloch 152s in service. But of this number only thirty-seven Bloch 151s and ninety-three Bloch 152s were actually operational.

GCI/1 was the first unit to receive Bloch 152s. The unit was supposed to receive a full complement of the aircraft, but did not receive all twenty-five until the end of October 1939. Eventually, by 10 May 1940, seven GC units had these aircraft. As soon as they encountered German aircraft the shortcomings of the Bloch 152 became readily apparent. It was incapable of flying fast enough or of climbing quickly enough. The propellers were unreliable; it had faulty radio equipment and range of just 360 miles.

On the up side, the Bloch 152 was manoeuvrable; it had two wing-mounted 20 mm canons and it was capable of taking a great deal of punishment. On one occasion a Bloch 152 returned to base with 360 bullet and cannon shell holes in its air frame.

Bloch fighter pilots shot down 146 German aircraft during the battle of France and these included many of the German front-line fighters. On the down side, 270 Bloch fighters were either shot down or had to be abandoned and forty of the pilots had been killed, plus forty-two of them wounded.

After the armistice Vichy France still had a number of Bloch fighters; in fact, 320 were on strength on 20 July 1940. They were being operated by six GC groups. When the Germans invaded Vichy France on 13 November 1942 the remaining 173 Blochs fell into German hands.

Arguably, the best French fighter of the Second World War was the Dewoitine 520. There were a number of false starts in its development from 1934. The designer, Émile Dewoitine, left his own company in June 1936 so that he could have a totally free hand at designing a revolutionary and modified aircraft. The designs were submitted in January 1937 and within two months the Air Ministry agreed that the aircraft would probably be ideal for their requirements. Detailed drawings were made, which prompted the construction of a prototype. It was delivered in November 1938. After looking at the full-scale mock-up and requesting some modifications, the final prototype was ready by the middle of January 1939. There were more tests and prototypes, which gradually improved the aircraft's design and performance.

The Air Ministry was, finally, suitably impressed and the initial contract was for 200 Dewoitine 520s to be delivered between September and December 1939. On 5 June 1939 another 600 were ordered (later reduced to 510 in the July). In September 1939 a third contract required 170 Dewoitine 520s. This now meant that the orders amounted to 880 machines. The production rate was to be 200 per month from May 1940. Subsequently, the contracts were amended so that 2,205 Dewoitine 520s would be produced at a rate of 350 per month from November 1940. This was in addition to 120 that had been ordered by the French navy.

The first group to switch over to the Dewoitine 520 was an MS406 unit, GCI/3, in November 1939. The unit was to be equipped with thirty-four of the aircraft by January 1940, but production delays meant that this was not achieved until the beginning of May.

When the Germans attacked Western Europe on 10 May 1940 some 246 Dewoitine 520s had been produced and the air force had accepted seventy-nine of them into service. The GCI/3 was deployed near Rheims on 11 May 1940 and, two days later, the Dewoitine 520 claimed its first set of kills when three HS126 reconnaissance aircraft and a He111 were shot down for no loss. On 15 May the Dewoitine 520s shot down four Bf110s, two Bf109s, two Do17s and a pair of He111s. However, two of the Dewoitine 520 pilots were lost in the engagement and two other pilots were wounded.

GCI/3 was down to six operational Dewoitine 520s by 16 May and it became more and more difficult to keep them operational as the unit shifted further into southern France during late May and early June. Nonetheless, by the time the armistice came into effect on

25 June the group had fifty confirmed kills and eighteen probable hits.

The combined score of the Dewoitine 520s during the battle of France amounted to 108 confirmed and thirty-nine probable hits. In exchange, 106 Dewoitine 520s had been lost but only twenty-six in air combat.

By June 1940 some 437 of the aircraft had been constructed, 351 had gone to the air force and fifty-two to the navy. However, by this time there were only 331 Dewoitine 520s left; 153 of them were in occupied France, three had been flown to England and 175 of them were in North Africa.

The Germans were suitably impressed with the Dewoitine 520 and placed an order of their own for 550 of them. The first twenty-two were delivered in August 1941. The contract was terminated when the 349th aircraft had been delivered to the Germans at the end of December 1942. By this stage, a total of 786 Dewoitine 520s had been manufactured.

Two fighter groups supplied with Dewoitine 520s and a naval squadron fought in Syria in the summer of 1941. For the loss of thirty-two aircraft, which included eleven in air combat, seven destroyed on the ground and fourteen abandoned, destroyed or stripped, they claimed thirty confirmed kills and six probable hits.

When Operation *Torch* was launched in November 1942 the Vichy Air Force had five GC units and two naval *escadrilles* with 173 Dewoitine 520s, of which 142 were operational. In the short campaign the Vichy forces lost thirty-five Dewoitine 520s, sixteen of which were air force aircraft and nineteen were naval machines.

When the Germans marched into unoccupied France and disbanded what remained of the Vichy Air Force, they seized 1,876 aircraft, of which 246 were Dewoitine 520s. They also captured 169 of the aircraft that were in various stages of completion at the Toulouse plant of the manufacturer.

Following the landings by the Allies in southern France in August 1944, a French interior force's fighter unit was created using re-captured Dewoitine 520s. Around fifty-five additional Dewoitine 520s were recovered as the Allies advanced towards Germany.

The Germans made good use of the captured Dewoitine 520s, sending sixty of them to Italy and then 100 to Bulgaria, where they were deployed by No. 6 Regiment. Many of these aircraft were subsequently shot down by the US 9th Air Force and the unit was re-equipped with Bf109s.

The last remaining Dewoitine 520s in French service comprised a presentation squadron, which was finally disbanded in September 1953.

Appendix 1

Armée de l'Air 1940

Northern France

The headquarters was based at St Jean-les-Deux-Jumeaux, under General Vuillemin. On strength were three Morane 406s, of which two were believed to be operational.

The north-east zone of operations, based at La Ferté-sous-Jouarre, was commanded by General Têtu. The northern area headquarters, under General d'Astier de la Vigerie, was based at Chauny. Neither of these headquarters was believed to have any attached aircraft.

The French had a number of fighter groups available to them in northern France. The first was *Groupement de Chasse* 21. In overall command was General Pinsard, based at Chantilly-les-Aigles. The group was given the task of the day defence of Paris. The group itself consisted of five GC units. GCI/1 had fifteen of its twenty-three Bloch 152s available, under *Commandant* Soviche at Chantilly-les-Aigles. GCII/1, also with Bloch 152s, was based at Buc, under *Commandant* Robillon and it was believed to have had eighteen of its twenty-five aircraft available. GCII/3 was undergoing re-equipment and was based at Beauvais-Tillé. It could muster twenty-three of its twenty-eight Morane 406s and half of the four Dewoitine 520s. GCII/10, under *Commandant* Ronzet, was based at Rouen-Boos and had a mix of Bloch 151s and 152s, with just twenty of the thirty-one available for action. At Le Havre, GCIII/10 also had Bloch 151s and 152s, but just eighteen of the thirty-nine aircraft were available for action.

For the most part, *Groupement de Chasse* 23 was in a slightly better state as far as aircraft were concerned. The group headquarters, under General Romatet, was based at Laon-Chambry with both of its Curtiss H75s. Also at the same base was GCII/2 with twenty-two of its twenty-six Morane 406s ready. At Cambrai-Niergnies, GCIII/2 had twenty-eight Morane 406s, but an additional six were not operational. GCI/4, at Wez-Thuisy, had all but one of its thirty Curtiss H75s ready. At the same base was ECMJ 1/16, with ten of its seventeen Potez 613s available. GCI/5, based at Suippes, could muster twenty-five of its twenty-nine Curtiss-aircraft.

Groupement de Chasse 25 was a far smaller force. Under Lieutenant Colonel de Moussac, it was based at Aire-sur-La-Lys. The two GC units, III/1 and II/8, had Morane 406 or Bloch 152 aircraft. The former was based at Norrent-Fontes with twenty of its thirty Moranes ready for action. The other unit with Blochs was at Calais-Marck with eleven of the nineteen aircraft serviceable.

The final fighter element comprised the night fighters of *Groupement de Chasse de Nuit*. They were based at Meaux-Esbly for the night defence of Paris. The unit was commanded by Lieutenant Colonel Dordilly. Posted to the same base was ECN1/13, with eight of its twelve Potez 631s available for action. The whole *groupement* was issued with Potez 631s. The other units were ECN2/13 at Melun-Villaroche with seven of eleven aircraft available, ECN3/13 at Le Plessis-Belleville with ten of twelve aircraft available and ECN4/14 at Betz-Bouillancy with seven of twelve aircraft available.

There were, of course, bomber units attached for operations in northern France. They were organized along with GRII/33, which was a reconnaissance unit. The reconnaissance unit itself was based at Athies-sous-Laon with a mixture of Potez 637s, Potez 63-11s and Bloch 174s. The other three squadrons, *Groupement de Bombardement* 6, 9 and *Groupement de Bombardement D'Assaut* 18, were spread out across northern France. *Groupement de Bombardement* 6 had its headquarters at Soissons where GBI/12 had nine of fourteen LeO451s available. The other unit, GBII/12, also with LeO451s, had all but one of its fourteen aircraft available at Persan-Beaumont. *Groupement de Bombardement* 9 had two GB units; I/34 was based at La Ferté-Gaucher and had ten of thirteen Amiot 143s and two of three Amiot 354s available. GBII/34, at Montdidier, had a mix of the 143s, 354s and Bloch 131s, of which only ten of the fifteen aircraft were ready for action. Also at La Ferté-Gaucher was GBI/54, belonging to *Groupement de Bombardement D'Assaut* 18, with all of its thirteen Breguet 693s ready. At Nangis the remaining unit of the group, GBII/54, had ten of the same aircraft ready.

The French Air Force also supplied a large number of reconnaissance and observation squadrons. These were attached specifically to French armies. The French 1st Army had access to eight
units of various sizes, with a mixture of different aircraft, including
Potez 63-11s, Mureaux 115s and LeOC30s; just fewer than seventy
aircraft in total were available to them. The French 2nd Army was
not so well served and could only call upon some forty-five aircraft
from five different groups. The 7th Army had the support of four
different groups, mainly Potez 63-11s and Mureaux 115s, with some
forty aircraft available. The 9th Army, again with mainly Potez
and Mureaux aircraft, comprised five groups with a total available
strength of just fewer than forty aircraft. There was also a small
reserve based at Connantre, with Potez and Mureaux aircraft, of
which only six of nine were available for action.

This whole northern zone found itself under particular pressure
from 3 June 1940, when the *Luftwaffe*, following the withdrawal of
British and Allied troops from Dunkirk, attempted to ensure air
supremacy by destroying what remained of the French Air Force.
The Germans launched 1,100 aircraft, including many bombers,
which were aiming to destroy the majority of French aircraft on the
ground. Although the French were aware of the attack around an
hour before it was launched, few of the French units managed to
scramble in time to intercept the incoming German aircraft. The
Germans would claim that the operation accounted for 400 French
aircraft on the ground and seventy-five in aerial combat. The true
figures are much more likely to be around twenty destroyed on the
ground and fifteen in dogfights.

Eastern France
The second major French formation covered the east and was
headquartered at Nancy, under General Bouscat. It, too, comprised
fighter squadrons and bomber squadrons, along with reconnaissance and observation squadrons. The single fighter group, *Groupement de Chasse* 22, under Colonel Dumèmes, was headquartered at
Velaine-en-Haye, with a handful of Morane 406s, Curtiss H75s
and Bloch 152s. The main units were comparatively strong. GCI/2
had twenty-seven of thirty-one Morane 406s ready for action at
Toul-Ochey. GCII/4, based at Xaffévillers had all-but two of its

thirty-one Curtiss H75s ready. GCII/5, at Toul-Croix-de-Metz, was less well prepared with just over half of its twenty-six Curtiss H75s ready. Both the GCII/6 and GCIII/7 had Morane 406 aircraft and, in theory, they should have mustered thirty-four aircraft. But, respectively, only twenty were ready at Anglure-Vouarces and twenty-three at Vitry le François-Vauclere. The remaining unit, GCI/8, had twenty of its thirty-seven Bloch 152s available at Velaine-en-Haye, where it was based with the headquarters of the group.

There was one *Groupement de Bombardement* under Lieutenant Colonel Aribaut (No 10). These were issued with Amiot 143s and Bloch 200s. The two units, GBI/38 and GBII/38, were based at Troyes-Barberey and Chaumont-Semoutiers respectively. Together, they could put twenty-two of their twenty-nine aircraft into the air. The second *Groupement de Bombardement* 15, under Colonel Moraglia, was based at Rheims. The two units, GBI/15 and GBII/15, both had Farman 222s but only six of the twenty aircraft were available.

Once again, the French Air Force made a number of reconnaissance and observation aircraft available to the army by specifically attaching them. The 3rd French Army had seven squadrons available to them. These had a mix of Potez 63-11s, 27s and 637s, as well as Mureaux 113s, 115s and 117s; a total of sixty aircraft were available. The 4th French Army could call on nine different squadrons, again with a mix of Potez and Mureaux aircraft and a handful of Curtiss 875s and Breguet 27s. Collectively, they could muster sixty-two aircraft. This part of the French Air Force took the brunt of the initial German attacks and had, of course, contributed to the air battles over Holland and other Low Countries.

Southern France
The units available to cover southern France were under General Odic's command. The fighter units were dotted around a number of bases, including Marseilles, Lyons and Corsica. Eight fighter squadrons were available and these had a variety of different aircraft, including Morane 406s, Bloch 151s and 152s, Potez 631s and Dewoitine 520s. Many of the figures of aircraft available are unknown or uncertain.

There were also units in the reconnaissance and army cooperation role. GRI/33, based at Dôle, could offer only a handful of Potez and Bloch aircraft. Three reconnaissance and observation squadrons were assigned to the 8th French Army, again with Potez and Bloch aircraft, mustering around twenty-two that were serviceable. There was also a small reserve at Romilly.

The Alps

The Alps region, under General Laurens, was based at Valence. *Groupement de Bombardement* 6, with two squadrons, was based at Lézignan with LeO451s and Bloch 210s, of which just thirteen of thirty-six were available for action. *Groupement de Bombardement* 7, at Istres, also had LeO451s and Bloch 210s, mustering a total of twenty-two aircraft. *Groupement de Bombardement* 9 at Avignon-Château-blanc mustered twenty-two Bloch 210s and Amiot 354s. *Groupement de Bombardement* 11 at Arles was in a similar position with twenty-eight of its fifty-one aircraft available for action. The final unit was *Groupement de Bombardement D'Assaut* 19, mainly based in Provence, with a combination of Breguet 691s and 693s. It was a very under-strength group of three squadrons, which probably could only muster around seventeen aircraft.

Two reconnaissance and observation squadrons were attached to the French Army of the Alps, although only around ten aircraft were readily available. There was also a small general reserve at Marcilloles and Montbard, with a paper strength of twenty aircraft, of which approximately thirteen were airworthy.

There were also a number of local defence flights. None of these were usually capable of mustering more than about half a dozen aircraft. These small defensive units were scattered around the country at bases such as Caen, Rennes, Toulouse and Tours. They had a wide variety of different aircraft, including some British and Italian models.

North Africa

The French took their defence of North Africa extremely seriously, with a number of fighter and bomber squadrons scattered throughout Algeria, Morocco and Tunisia. Paradoxically, it would be many of these aircraft and those further afield that would see action as part of the Vichy air force. This could also be said of what remained of the French Air Force, particularly in the southern part of mainland France.

Algeria had two fighter squadrons, GCI/6 and GCI/10, based at Oran. It is not known exactly how many aircraft were available. Morocco had two squadrons, ERC571 and ERC573, both at Casablanca. These had been issued with Dewoitine 510s and had strength on paper of twenty aircraft. In Tunisia, based at Sidi-Ahmed, there were two fighter squadrons, ERC572 and ERC474, with Morane 406s and Spad 510s.

There were also bomber units in North Africa. Morocco had the biggest concentration with GBII/62, GBII/63, GBI/19, GBII/19 and GBII/61. These had been issued with Glenn Martin 617Fs, Bloch 210s and Douglas DB7s. Theoretically, each of the units would have had up to a dozen or so aircraft. Tunisia had a single Bloch 200 squadron, GBI/25, based with the fighters at Sidi-Ahmed. In Algeria, GBII/25, with LeO257bis, was based at Bougie.

There were also reconnaissance and observation squadrons scattered far and wide across the three countries. Unfortunately, we only know a little about their strength, which seemed to fluctuate from between four and a dozen aircraft. The majority of these aircraft were Potez 25s, 29s and 63-11s. Morocco had five of these squadrons, Algeria six and Tunisia had just two.

The Middle East
There was just a single fighter squadron based at Rayak in the Lebanon. This was GCI/7 with a paper strength of twenty-six Morane 406s. At the same base were a dozen Glenn Martin 167Fs of GBI/39.

In Syria there were a dozen Potez 63-11s of GRII/39 and half a dozen of the same aircraft belonging to GAO1/583.

Further Potez 25 and 29 reconnaissance and observation squadrons, each with a strength of around six aircraft, were also available. There were four more in Syria and just one in Lebanon.

Indochina
The French Air Force had a mixed bag of aircraft scattered across Indochina. French Indochina was a sprawling area and was served

by just seven units. On paper, the squadrons could muster between four and ten aircraft each. Spare parts, however, were a major issue; hence it is very difficult to know precisely how many of these aircraft were airworthy. Predominantly, the units in areas such as Cambodia, Tonkin and Annam were issued with Potez 25 aircraft.

East and West Africa
French Somalia had a small air detachment of Potez 25s, 29s and 631s based at Djibouti, where it is believed that there were eighteen aircraft. In French West Africa, principally in Senegal, there were two small units issued with Potez 25s, 542s, Farman 222s and Dewoitine 501s. It is believed that around fifteen aircraft were available.

The remaining and most remote French outpost in Africa was actually off the main continent, on Madagascar. There was a small unit of ten Potez 25 and 29s at Ivato.

Appendix 2

Vichy Air Force – September 1940

Under the terms of the armistice, the French Air Force was forced to set the limit on the size of its fighter squadrons to twenty-six aircraft, while its reconnaissance and bomber squadrons could have thirteen aircraft.

Unoccupied France
Nine fighter squadrons were still in existence in the unoccupied zone of France, the majority of them were equipped with Bloch 152s, some with Potez 631s and one squadron G I/6 with Morane 406s. The deployment of the squadrons can be seen below:

GC I/1	Lyon-Bron
GC II/1	Le Luc-en-Provence
GC I/6	Salon-de-Provence
GC I/8	Montpellier-Fréjorgues
GC I/8	Marignane
GC II/9	Aulnat
GC III/9	Salon-de-Provence
ECN I/13	Nimes-Garons
ECN III/13	Nimes-Garons

The seven bomber squadrons were based either at Istres or Lézignan. They had a mix of different aircraft as can be seen in the table below:

GBI/12	Lioré et Olivier LéO 451
GBII/15	Farman F 222
GBI/31	Lioré et Olivier LéO 451

GBI/38	Amiot 143
GBI/38	Amiot 143
GBAI/51	Bréguet 693 and Bréguet 695
GBAI/54	Bréguet 693

There were just three reconnaissance squadrons in unoccupied France, based at Perpignan (GRI/14), Avignon (GRII/14) and Montpellier (GRII/22). All were equipped with Potez 63-11 aircraft.

North Africa
The Vichy were much better served in North Africa, with a number of French aircraft having made the journey across the Mediterranean to then be incorporated into squadrons in North Africa.

The GC units were fighter squadrons and the bomber squadrons GB units. Reconnaissance units had the GR identification.

In Algeria there were:

GCI/3	Oran-La Sénia	Dewoitine 520
GCII/3	Alger-Maison Blanche	Dewoitine 520
GCIII/6	Alger-Maison Blanche	Dewoitine 520
GBI/11	Oran-Saint-Denis-du-Sig	Lioré et Olivier LéO 451
GBI/19	Sétif	Douglas DB-7
GBII/25	Bougie	Lioré et Olivier LéO H 257 bis (*later* Lioré et Olivier LéO 451)
GBII/61	Blida	Douglas DB-7
GRI/36	Sétif	Potez 63-11
GRI/52	Oran-La Sénia	Potez 63-11
GRII/52	Oran-La Sénia	Bloch 175

In Morocco there were:

GCI/5	Rabat-Salé	Curtiss H-75
GCII/5	Casablanca	Curtiss H-75
GBI/23	Meknès	Lioré et Olivier LéO 451
GBII/23	Meknès	Lioré et Olivier LéO 451
GBI/32	Camp Cazès	Douglas DB-7
GBII/32	Agadir	Douglas DB-7
GBII/63	Marrakech	Martin 167 F
GRI/22	Rabat-Salé	Martin 167 F

Tunisia had considerably fewer units available:

GCII/7	Sidi-Ahmed	Dewoitine 520
GBI/15	Thélepte	Farman F 222
GBI/25	Tunis-El Aouina	Lioré et Olivier LéO 451

Middle East

In the Middle East, there was just one fighter and one bomber squadron, both of which were based in Lebanon. There were eight reconnaissance and observation squadrons split between Syria and Lebanon.

GCI/7	Rayack	Morane 406
GBI/39	Baalbeck	Martin 167 F

In Lebanon, there was just one reconnaissance and observation squadron (Esc3/39 based at Rayack, equipped with Bloch 200s). The remainder were all in Syria, equipped either with Potez 63-11s or Potez 25TOEs.

GRII/39	Damas-Mezzé
GAO1/583	Alep-Nerab
EO592	Rayack
EO593	Alep-Nerab
EO594	Damas-Mezzé
EO595	Palmyre
EO596	Deir el Zor

French West Africa

In French West Africa, the squadrons were all based in Senegal. The solitary fighter squadron was at Dakar (GCI/4) and had Curtiss H-75s. There were three bomber squadrons (GBI/62, GBII/62 and GBI/63), all based at Thiès and all equipped with Martin 167Fs. In addition to this there was an autonomous squadron with a mix of Farman and Potez aircraft at the same base.

Madagascar

There was just one squadron based in Madagascar (EO555), with Potez 25TOEs.

French Somalia
At Djibouti, there was a detachment of Potez 25TOEs, Potez 63-11 and Potez 29s.

Indochina
There were four commands in Indochina. *Groupe Aérien Autonome* 41, consisted of ER1/41 and EB2/41, which were equipped with Potez 25TOEs and Farman 221s respectively at Pusat in Cambodia and Tong in Tonkin. *Groupe Aérien Autonome* 42 (ER1/42 and EB2/42) was at Pusat in Cambodia and Tan Son Nut in Cochin China with Potez 25TOEs and Potez 542s. *Groupe Aérien Mixte* 595 (EO1/595 and EC2/595) with Potez 25TOEs and Morane 406s were at Dong Hoi in Annam and Bach Mai in Tonkin. The final unit, *Groupe Aérien Mixte* 596 (EO1/596 and Esc1/CBS), was equipped with Potez 25TOEs and Loire
130s, based at Tourane and Da Nang in Annam and Cat Lai in Cochin China.

Appendix 3

Vichy Air Force Victory Credits

Rank	First Name	Surname	Victories	Total	Units	Death	Note
Lt	Pierre	LE GLOAN	7	18	GCIII/6	11/09/1943	D-520 ace, France, Syria.
Cap	Georges	BLANCK	6	12	GCII/3, GCI/3, GCIII/3, GC1/3 'Corse'	08/01/1990	Battle of France, Algeria, Corsica, 40–43.
Capt	Leon (Jacques)	RICHARD	6	6	GCIII/6	26/05/1943	Vichy AF ace, Syria 41. KIFA.
A/C	Jean	DUGOUJON	4	6	GCII/5, GCI/3		
Cne	Roger	DUVAL	4	8	GCIII/3, GC1/3 'Nice'		Spitfire, Corsica, 1943.
Lt	Michel	MADON	4	11	GCI/3, GCIII/3, GCII/7, GCI/7	16/05/1972	D-520, Battle of France, Vichy, Corsica.
Lt	George	PISSOTTE	4	8	GC III/2, GCIII/3, GCI/3		
Capt	Pierre	POUPART	4	4	GCIII/3, GCI/3		D-520.
EV	Jacques	DU MERLE	3	3	Esc.1AC	12/03/1943	*Aéronavale* pilot, Syria, 1941.
Capt	Robert	HUVET	3	8	GCII/5	08/11/1942	Battle of France, Syria.
Lt	Marcel	STEUNOU	3	5	GCIII/6	23/06/1941	MS-406, Levant, 1941.
A/C	Georges	AMARGER	2	3	GCI/7, GCII/7		
A/C	Paul	BAILLET	2	2	GCI/4		H-75, defence of Dakar, 1940.

163

Rank	First Name	Surname	Victories	Total	Units	Death	Note
Sgt	Louis	COISNEAU	2	3	GCII/4, GCIII/6	03/02/1943	D.520, Syria 41.
S/Lt	Georges	ELMLINGER	2	8	GC III/2, GCIII/6, GCIII/3		D.520, Syria 41.
SC	Justin 'Jean'	GISCLON	2	5	GCII/5		*Aéronavale* pilot, Levant, 1941.
PM	Paul	GOFFENY	2	2	Esc.AC1	01/01/1945	
SC	André	LEGRAND	2	9	GCII/5		Hawk-75, Battle of France, defence of Morocco.
SC	Jean	MACCIA	2	2	GCIII/6		D.520, Syria, 1941.
S/Lt	Gabriel	MERTZISEN	2	7	GCIII/6, GC3 'Normandie'	30/09/1951	D.520, Syria 41.
Sgt	Alain 'Papichou'	MICHAUX	2	2	GCIII/6		D.520, Syria, 1941.
Lt	Pierre	MINOT	2	3	GCI/4		H-75, Dakar, 1940.
Lt	George	PATIN	2	2	GCII/3		
S/Lt	Georges	RIVORY	2	2	GCIII/6		
Adj	Daniel	RONCIN	2	2	GCIII/3		
S/Lt	Georges	RUCHOUX	2	5	GCII/5		
Lt	Marie-Henri	SATGÉ	2	5	GCIII/6	30/09/1943	
Cdt	Georges	TRICAUD	2	5	GCI/6, GCII/5	08/11/1942	'Vichy Air Force' ace.
Lt	Paul	ABRIOUX	1	5	GCIII/1	17/11/1951	Battle of France, Morocco.
S/Lt	Jacques	ANDRÉ	1	16	GCII/3, GC3 'Normandie'	02/04/1988	Battle of France, Syria, N. Africa, Russia.
PM	Raymond	BEDARD	1	2	AC2, GCII/7	*Aéronavale* pilot. Morocco 42. Germany 44.	
PM	Jean	BENEZET	1	1	1AC		D.520, 1941.
Lt	Emile	BOIRIES	1	1	GCIII/6	18/06/1941	D.529, Syria 41, KIA.
S/Lt	Paul	BOUDIER	1	4	GCII/5		
Sgt	Andre	BOUHY	1	5	GCII/5		Battle of France, Morocco.
Adj	Jeremie	BRESSIEUX	1	9	GCI/5	08/11/1942	Battle of France, N. Africa, Alsace.

Rank	First Name	Surname	Victories	Total	Units	Death	Note
Capt	Guillaume	DE RIVALS-MAZÈRES	1	1	GCIII/6, CEAM Orléans		D.520, test pilot, 1940.
A/C	Raymond	DELANNOY	1	1	GCII/5	15/01/1943	
Cdt	Louis	DELFINO	1	15	GCI/4, GCII/9, GC3 'Normandie'	11/06/1968	Battle of France, Russian front.
S/Lt	Jean	DUSSART	1	3	GCII/7		
Cdt	Guy	FANNEAU DE LA HORIE	1	1	GCI/4	25/08/1944	H-75, Dakar, 1940.
S/C	Marcel	FARRIOL	1	1	GCIII/6		H-75, Dakar 1940.
Cne	André	GAUTHRIN	1	2	GCI/4		D.520, Syria, 1941.
Sgt	Henri 'Achille'	GHESQUIERE	1	1	GCIII/6		
Sgt	Jean	HURTIN	1	6	GCIII/3, GCII/3, GCI/4	23/02/1944	
Adj	Marcel	JEANNAUD	1	5	GCIII/3, GCII/3		Morocco 1942. Defected to Germany.
Sgt	René	LAVIE	1	1	GCII/5		
Lt	Yves	LE CALVEZ	1	4	GCI/5		
Lt	Guy	LE STUM	1	2	GCII/5	27/12/1943	
Lt	Marcel Emile Marie	LEBLANC	1	7	GCIII/3, GCII/3	28/01/1944	
Lt	Georges	LEGRAND	1	2	GCIII/6		
S/Lt	Georges	LEMARE	1	13	GCI/4, GC3 'Normandie'	26/01/1948	Battle of France, Defence of Dakar, Russian front.
Cne	François	LEONETTI	1	1	GAM Madagascar		MS.406 Madagascar 1942.
S/Lt	Charles	LEROY	1	4	GCIII/3, GCI/7		
Lt	René	LETE	1	1	GCII/3		
SC	Martin	LOI	1	5	GCII/3, GCIII/6 Vichy	27/07/1943	Vichy D.520 ace. KIFA.
Sgt	Jean	MEQUET	1	1	GCIII/6		
A/C	Jean	MONCHANIN	1	2	GCI/1, GCI/5		

Rank	First Name	Surname	Victories	Total	Units	Death	Note
Cdt	Marie	MONRAISSE	1	7	GCII/5, GCI/5, 3Esc, 1Esc	08/10/1944	
S/C	Pierre	MONRIBOT	1	2	GCIII/2		
SM	Robert	MOULINIER	1	2	AB2, Flotille 1F 2AC		Aéronavale pilot, Maroc, 1942.
Cne	Patrick	O'BYRNE	1	1	GCI/4		H-75, Dakar, 1940.
LV		PIREL	1	1	1F		D.520, Levant, 1941.
Capt	Marcel	ROUQUETTE	1	10	GCI/5		Curtiss H-75, Battle of France ace, N. Africa, Mediterranean Theatre of Operations.
Lt	Yves	RUPIED	1	2	GCIII/7, GCI/4		
A/C	Marcel	SAINTE MARIE	1	1	GCIII/3		
Sgt	Alain	SAVINEL	1	1	GCIII/6	23/06/1941	D.520, Syria, 1941, KIA.
Lt		THOMAS	1	1	GCI/4	13/08/1942	
Capt	Georges	VALENTIN	1	11	GCI/2, GCII/7	08/09/1944	MS-406 Battle of France; D.520: Spitfire, 1943.
Lt	Pierre	VILLACEQUE	1	6	GCII/5, GC1/3 'Corse'	14/05/2002	
S/Lt	André	VUILLEMAIN	1	1	GCI/7		
Adj	Leon	VUILLEMAIN	1	11	GCI/5	10/10/1974	Curtiss H-75, Battle of France.

Appendix 4

Vichy Air Force in Indochina

In May 1940 *Groupe Aérien Autonome* 41 had a total strength of around thirteen aircraft. By September of the same year the group was believed to be considerably weaker, but throughout the whole of Indochina there were around thirty Potez 25s available.

Groupe Aérien Autonome 42 had around sixteen aircraft available in May 1940. Figures for September 1940 seem to suggest that this had dropped to fewer than ten serviceable aircraft.

Groupe Aérien Mixte 595 had seven Potez 25s available to them in May 1940 and around sixteen by the September.

Groupe Aérien Mixte 596 had just six Potez 25s in May, but thirteen were available to them in the September, including seven Morane 406s. In fact, the Moranes, strictly speaking, were not available in September 1940, as Esc2/696 was only created in the October. In addition, there were twelve aircraft available to Esc1/CBS in May 1940.

Three Potez 631C were purchased by China (those with C designation). The aircraft were impounded in Hai Phong. It is believed that two of the aircraft were used for reconnaissance missions until around 1943. The third aircraft was used for spare parts. It is probable that of the two used aircraft one was used by the squadron commander of GAA41 and the other by the squadron commander of GAA42. The Morane 406s that were part of 596 were originally due to be sold to the Chinese, but they were also impounded.

The *Aéronautique Navale*'s EscHS6, based at Cat-Laï, had Loire 130s, Gourdou-Leseurre 832s and Potez 452s, amounting to eight aircraft in total. The Loire 130s were seaplanes and predominantly used for night missions and fitted with anti-submarine bombs. By June 1941, it is believed that there were nineteen Morane 406s left in Indochina. Seven of the Morane 406s were with *Escadrille* 2/595, an additional six flying with *Escadrille* 2/596. It is believed that the remainder were in the repair pool and being used for spare parts.

The Franco–Thai War (1940–1941)

The *Armée de l'Air* had, theoretically, around a hundred aircraft available for this conflict. The front-line aircraft amounted to some sixty aircraft of a variety of types including:

- thirty Potez 25 TOEs
- four Farman 221s
- six Potez 542s
- nine Morane-Saulnier M.S.406
- eight Loire 130 flying boats

The Royal Thai Air Force could muster around 140 aircraft, comprising:

- twenty-four Mitsubishi Ki-30 light bombers
- nine Mitsubishi Ki-21 medium bombers
- twenty-five Hawk 75Ns pursuit planes
- six Martin B-10 medium bombers
- seventy O2U Corsair light bombers

During the war with Thailand, the French launched just over 190 day missions and just over fifty night missions. The conflict ended on 28 January 1941. It had led to a number of key servicing problems for the aircraft. There were still nineteen French Moranes, of which only fourteen were serviceable. In addition, the French still had three serviceable Farman 221s, three out of four Potez 542s, only thirty-four of their fifty-four Potez 25s, nine of their twelve Loire 130s and none of their three Potez 631s available.

At the end of the hostilities, the German Armistice Commission allowed the transfer of aircraft reinforcements to Indochina. The Commission authorized the following aircraft to be transferred from Martinique:

- twenty-three Hawk H-75s
- forty-four Curtiss SBC-4s

However, the Japanese resisted this transfer and the plans to move the aircraft from Martinique were cancelled. As a result, *Escadrille*

2/596 was disbanded due to lack of spare parts for its aircraft and what remained of the unit, including both the pilots and the aircraft, were transferred to *Escadrille* 2/595. This disbandment and transfer took place in the middle of 1941.

Vichy Air Force in Indochina – January 1942

Throughout 1942 there had been a major reorganization in Indochina. Operating out of Tong in Tonkin were both units of the newly created Northern Indochina Air Command, consisting of *Groupement Mixte* 1 and 2. The first unit had Farman 221s and Potez 542s and the second had Potez 25s and Morane 406s. The second grouping, Central Indochina Air Command, consisted of an observation unit based at Bach Mai in Tonkin and equipped with Potez 25s. *Groupe Aérien Mixte* 4, based at Dong Hoy in Annam and at Vatchay in Cambodia, had Potez 25s and Loire 130s. Unfortunately, we do not know the strength of these units at this time. More reliable figures are available for November 1942, when the total strength of Northern Indochina Air Command amounted to eighteen aircraft. Central Indochina Air Command could muster twenty-nine aircraft.

By the end of 1942, the Vichy Air Force in Indochina had been reduced to the following:

- three Farman 221s
- two Potez 542s
- eighteen Potez 25TOEs
- seven Loire 130s

Appendix 5

Aéronautique Navale

This was, in effect, the French equivalent of the Fleet Air Arm. Although not strictly speaking within the scope of this book, there were obvious occasions when these units found themselves facing Allied aircraft.

French maritime aviation dates back to 1910. In 1912, the Department of Marine Aviation was created. At the outbreak of the First World War it was still a tiny force, with just twenty-six pilots and fourteen seaplanes. The service expanded considerably during the First World War and was involved in operations against enemy ships and submarines. Between 1910 and 1918, some 3,000 aircraft were used by the French marine aviation units, with an average service history of just six months per aircraft. By the end of the First World War the service had around 700 seaplanes.

There were considerable numbers of aircraft and units available in May 1940. As far as the German invasion of Western Europe was concerned, the two most important zones of combat for the French *Aéronautique Navale* were the northern and Atlantic zones and the Mediterranean zone. There were, of course, smaller formations scattered around the Middle East, French West Africa, the French West Indies and the Far East. In addition to the aircraft operating out of seaplane bases, there were others that operated from surface vessels.

Broadly speaking, the organization of the *Aéronautique Navale* was somewhat similar to the French Air Force itself. However, there were notable exceptions in as much as the *Aéronautique Navale* had separate torpedo and dive-bomber flights. They also designated aircraft for short-range patrols and for long-range patrols.

In terms of the squadrons themselves, although marked as *escadrilles*, they were organized into flotillas, particularly the fighters and the bombers. In the northern and Atlantic zone, the main base was at Calais, where *Flotille de Chasse* F1C had twenty-five Potez 631s available to them.

The bombers were based at Lanvéoc-Poulmic, where they have fourteen LeOH257bis. There were two torpedo flights of Latécoère 298s at Cherbourg, with twenty aircraft in total and a further ten at Boulogne. Also at Cherbourg, were Loire-Nieuport 411s, which were dive-bombers, with an additional twenty-four dive-bombers at Berck and Alprech.

Short-range surveillance flight patrol aircraft operated out of Cherbourg, St Trojan, Saint-Nazaire, Escoublac and Deauville. Long-range reconnaissance ·patrol aircraft were all based at Lanvéoc-Poulmic.

In the Mediterranean zone there was only one fighter flight, comprising Dewoitine 510s and Bloch 151s, based at Hyères-Le Palyvestres. There were no bombers, but there were ten torpedo Latécoère 298s at Berre and thirteen Vought 156Fs at Hyères-Le Palyvestres.

Both the short- and long-range patrol aircraft were split between the French mainland, Corsica, Algeria, Tunisia and Morocco. The short-range patrol aircraft were a mixed bag of different models, based at Hyères-Le Palyvestres, St Mandrier and Berre on the French mainland, Aspretto on Corsica, Karouba in Tunisia, Arzew in Algeria and Goulimine in Morocco.

Further afield, in Africa and based at Dakar in Senegal, were seven aircraft. There were just six Loire 130s in Tripoli in the Lebanon and a further seven in Martinique in the French West Indies. The furthest posted unit was in the Pacific Ocean, on Tahiti.

To add to the strength of the squadrons in North Africa, there were also shipborne aircraft based at Karouba in Tunisia and others at Arzew in Algeria. Across the fleet of vessels a number of Loire 130s were deployed, as were Gourdou-Leseurre 832s. These were mainly assigned to battleships and first- and second-class cruisers.

Bibliography

Bond, Peter, *The Third Century 1904–2004. 300 Years of British Gibraltar, 1704–2004*. Peter-Tan Publishing, 2003.

Brown, A.B., *History of the SA Air Force in World War II*, Vol. 4. Purnell, 1974.

Buckley, Christopher, *Five Ventures*, Her Majesty's Stationery Office, 1954.

Clayton, Colonel J.A., 'The South African Air Force in the Madagascar Campaign 1942', *Military History Journal*, Vol. 9, No. 2, South African Military History Society, 1992.

Ellis, Major L.F., *The War in France and Flanders*, Her Majesty's Stationery Office, 1953.

Fridenson, Patrick and Jean Lecuir, *La France et la Grande Bretagne face aux problèmes aériens*, Service Historique de l'Armée, 1976.

Green, William, *Warplanes of the Second World War, Vol. 2, Fighters*, Doubleday, 1961.

Green, William, *The Warplanes of the Third Reich*, Doubleday, 1970.

Herington, John, *Australia in the War of 1939 to 1945, Series 3 – Air – Volume III – Air War Against Germany and Italy 1939 to 1943*, Australian War Memorial, 1954.

Jackson, Robert, *Air War over France*, Ian Allen, 1974.

Joslen, H.F., *Orders of Battle*, Her Majesty's Stationery Office, 1960.

Kirby, S. Woodburn, *History of the Second World War: The War against Japan*, Vol. II, Her Majesty's Stationery Office, 1958.

Long, Gavin, *Australia in the War of 1939 to 1945, Series 1 – Army – Volume II – Greece, Crete and Syria*, Australian War Memorial, 1953.

Martin, H.J. and Neil D. Orpen, *South African Forces World War II, Vol. VII: South Africa at War*, Purnell, 1979.

Munson, Kenneth, *Fighters between the Wars 1919–1939*, Macmillan, 1970.

Munson, Kenneth, *Bombers between the Wars 1919–1939*, Macmillan, 1970.

Rohwer, J. and G. Hummelchen, *Chronology of the War at Sea, 1939-1945*, Naval Institute Press, 1992.

Van Haute, André, *Pictorial History of the French Air Force*, Ian Allen, 1974.

Wood, Derek and Derek Dempster, *The Narrow Margin*, Paperback Library, 1969.

Woodburn-Kirby, S., *History of the Second World War: UK Military Series The War against Japan*, Vol. II, Chap. 8, Her Majesty's Stationery Office, 1958.